CW01666714

Annihilate Social Anxiety - for Teens

Dr Thashna Walsh

ISBN - 978-1-915871-01-5

Contents

Acknowledgments 9
Foreword 11
Introduction 15

1. HOW YOUR MIND WORKS 27
Ways of the subconscious and conscious mind
What you believe, is your experience 32
How do I really feel about things? 36
It's all about the vibes 39

2. THE MANY FACES OF ANXIETY 51
What is anxiety
Types of Anxiety 58
Why are some people anxious, but others aren't? 69
Protect me, punish me or give me attention 70

3. WHAT IS SOCIAL ANXIETY? 75
Why do I feel this way?
Signs and symptoms 77
Causes and triggers 79
Other contributory factors 84

4. THE BATTLE FOR YOUR MIND 93
Realistic thinking trumps fear
Rules of the battlefield 97
Win the battle 102

5. STRATEGISE TO OVERCOME 111
The Coping Skills Toolkit
Affirm it 112
Caring what YOU think 116
Seek out the fear 120
Dancing with fear 123

6. A WHOLESOME LIFE FOR POSITIVE CHANGE 131
Adjust your lifestyle
Diet: 'Eat right' 131
Physical exercise: 'Get up, move your body and energise 139
Breathing 143
Sleep: 'Charge your battery' 153
Being social with a purpose 161

7. REWIRE AND FIRE 167
Banish Social Anxiety
The solutions 171
Annihilate fear and self-doubt 176
Transforming the discomfort 178
Mindfulness 180
Self-love 183
Self Hypnosis 188

8. THASHNA WALSH LIFESTYLE THERAPY (TWLT) 193
About RTT 194

Conclusion 197
About Author 203
Power Tools 207
Resources and Notes 209

A FREE GIFT FOR OUR READERS

WHAT YOU WILL GET:

- **BONUS EBOOK** - 7 ESSENTIAL LIFE SKILLS ALL TEENAGERS NEED TO KNOW NOW
- **BONUS MEDITATION** - RELAXING GUIDED MEDITATION CALLED "RELAX AND REWIRE"

To get exclusive access to these FREE bonus offers go to

https://www.thashnawalsh.com/free-bonus-content

My first short book Confidence Reload was dedicated to my one-year-old granddaughter Marley-Rae. My daughter Zoe was happy, of course, but she expressed that she was shocked she 'did not make the cut'. While writing this book, she said to me, "I hope this one is dedicated to me, mom!"

Yes, it is my beautiful bold bossy daughter. I am so proud of your outspokenness and your fantastic sense of humour. You are the teenager I raised that has blossomed into a mighty force of love, drive, fun, compassion and pure fire. Thank you for inspiring me every day to be more, do more, and keep shining. I love the way you own your life.

Acknowledgments

Andrew, my love, thank you for your unrelenting support and love. For the loving and caring space you have created and provided for me to bring this message to fruition. You have been so gentle and kind, and encouraging. I am so blessed to have you in my life. Thank you for your wonderful heart.

Zoe, my daughter and friend, you are so bold and free in your spirit. Your focus, drive and insights are inspiring. Thanks for the laughs along the journey. I am very proud of you.

Marley Rainbow, my GG, you are still the most confident one I know.

My Teachers in life: The past traumas; the ones that contributed to it and the ones that nurtured me back to the wholeness of thinking, thank you. Thank you Grandma Murley Smith, Mommy, Aunty Dorrel, Aunt Sweedie, Aunty Nurline, Cuz P.J. Wayne, Rita, Janine, Jojo and Janjan, for your impactful acts of love and words of wisdom and inspiration.

Thank you to all my friends and family that believe in me and are there for me. I love you all and deeply appreciate you.

Foreword

Dr. Thashna Walsh creatively and wisely approaches a subject that clearly identifies a path and remedy for what so many have fallen short of demonstrating. By utilising her own learned life experience and studies, she has captured the moments of transformation in the social, psychological and spiritual development of youth that many ignore, or refuse to face.

Anxiety and fear are the twins that can utterly disarm dreams, visions and futures, and often go unnoticed and undetected, often being assessed as normal growth challenges, but are clearly the destroyers of faith and courage in so many.

By focusing on what lies beyond increased stress and anxiety levels, Dr. Thashna marvellously charts a path for recovery, confidence and improved personal development and relationships. As complex as the subconscious and conscious mind can be to both understand and study, it is where Dr. Thashna begins to unravel the rhymes and reasons for human behaviour, she also unravels situations, traumas that can easily be transformed to influence the rise of productivity and health.

The battle is always in the mind, and Dr.Thashna, proposes and recommends solutions and strategies that deal with the challenges and victories of the youth as they discover who they are, and what their greatest battles may be. It is in the mind that our fears, faith and optimism all cohabit. She teaches us how to target the power of the mind to produce and strategise positive outcomes and coping skills, rather than give in to the overwhelming mismanagement of thoughts and doubt.

This book reaches the entire spectrum of human development and goes beyond just youth development. To read Annihilate Social Anxiety for Teens, is to learn more about ourselves, and how we operate. It teaches us that our past childhood may have been painful, confusing and heartbreaking, but we can still learn from them and be elevated by those lessons to greater confidence, greater communication, to become a greater you!

Once we know the truth about the weakness and inabilities of anxiety to achieve its goal of preventing substantive growth, we also learn that the answer to every challenge is knowledge, to know how to fix it. Dr. Thashna brilliantly uses her knowledge and reveals in these pages that while it's challenging for all of us. By understanding our past, while retraining our minds, we will rise and conquer, leaving the past of anxiety behind to walk strong and unshakable into an incredible future. I know you will love the work Dr Thashna has put together here. I have been blown away by it for certain. Free yourself from the thief of your dreams and get doing what you were born to do.

— **PJ Edmund, Sr. D.D, D.H.L., Bishop & Senior Pastor** -
Timbrel Church International, Inc.
author of *Be Positive: Keep a Word of Faith in Your Mouth*

Introduction

If you only knew you had superpowers like Professor X from the X-Men, making you capable of crushing and annihilating the anxiety you feel forever!

"It's like a constant fear of being perceived, watched and judged. I can't help but think that I'm a terrible person and that something must be wrong with me. It's no use trying to make friends because I know I'll get nervous and stammer when I talk. I really don't want to be 'that weirdo' or give a bad impression. I have zero friends and no one to talk to at school, which is embarrassing. What if everyone thinks I'm just some random loner?"

"I practise saying 'present!' for roll call before school every morning because speaking up in front of other people terrifies me. I hide in the bathroom or library between classes, so I don't have to walk in

the crowded hallways or talk to anyone outside. I avoid grabbing lunch from the cafeteria because there are so many people. Instead, I'll just grab whatever I can from the kitchen at home whilst leaving the house and sneak into a maintenance closet or a toilet cubicle at school to hide at lunchtime. It's very tiring, but I've had to learn these ways to be comfortable, to cope, you know? I just feel like I don't belong anywhere."

"I've never shopped for my own clothes; my mom gets them for me. I hate going to the mall. It's loud, people stare, and I feel like they are talking about me. When I see and hear a group of people laughing, I feel like they're laughing at me. I also don't want to run into anyone I know there. My heart beats pretty fast when the phone rings, and I usually let it go to voicemail and reply later in a text. Everyone says these are the 'wonder years' of my life. Well, it feels pretty bleak and dull right about now. I feel like I'm missing out on my life. I feel scared all the time I am out in social settings. Remember when you were little, and your mom would leave you in line at the cashier to go get something? The panic you'd feel at that moment of being left alone? Or the awkwardness and panic of having to give a presentation to your class. Imagine that panic, that constant thumping in your chest that tenses you up inside, messing with your mind whenever you go out to eat, shop or go on a walk. That's how I feel every time I have to step into social situations."

That's what social anxiety can look and feel like for some people. That's how it felt for me, for the most part. Did you notice the pattern of avoidance? Going to lengths to avoid people, places, and social situations for a feeling of safety is classic behaviour in social anxiety.

You're currently in an uneasy transition from a carefree childhood to those years when you have to start figuring things out for yourself, including figuring out yourself and your identity. You are expected to grow up, yet you are not given the tools or the freedom to do so, nor do you feel ready. It feels like sometimes you're between a rock and a hard place. Teenage years for many of us are marked by social awkwardness, which is the bitter cherry on top of a confusing mountain of other struggles at the time. It makes things more challenging than they already are. So it only makes sense that you want to retreat and avoid what makes you uncomfortable.

You feel this gaping void, this disconnection and discomfort because human beings are wired to seek connections with others. We aren't made to be alone. We have relied on each other to cooperate, take care of one another, and interact in ways that will help us survive for as long as possible. People need people. The feeling of being accepted is essential for thriving in life. On the other hand, when you think others don't like you, it can feel unsafe, and you feel more vulnerable to your fears of rejection and embarrassment. That's where the need to fit in comes from. You are generally likely to feel safer and more secure with a friend or a group of people you know who will accept you for who you are. When there's a lack of acceptance and validation, you start to feel somewhat alienated.

Given the COVID-19 situation that put the world on hold and changed life for everyone, lots of teens missed out on many opportunities in school. One of the many ways COVID impacted many teens was by knocking their confidence and self-esteem. There isn't an equivalent setting that exposes a teen to the real world like the social environment schools provide. When that was taken away, there was less space to grow in and grow through.

Social anxiety makes it difficult to make friends because your fears grip you tightly. It gets in the way of connecting with others and weighs down on you until you sink into hiding away from social environments.

Managing your school work and maintaining a social life has got to be one of life's great balancing acts. The clock is ticking, and it feels like there isn't enough time in the day. Some people don't dare to say "no" to plans even when they have a lot on their plate. They might fear letting the other person down, being seen as not 'fun enough', being let go of, or losing someone's interest. When the college you get into and the future of your career depend on the grades in your exams, everything else in life, including your social life, can feel secondary if you aren't good at balancing the two. All this balancing and time management is very stressful.

Then you have your parents, who, much like the other adults in your life, can only try so hard to help you, to the point that it becomes frustrating for you and them. Although well-intended, receiving empty advice from most grown-ups like "just be yourself!" or "you just need to put yourself out there!" could not feel more dismissive. What does this even mean? What if you don't want to "be yourself" because you don't like yourself? What if you can't "put yourself out there" because you feel like you aren't ready or don't even know how to do so? Why go 'out there' and risk embarrassment and failure when you can just stay in your safety bubble? What's the point, right? How will saying things like this help?

You will know the feeling of 'not being good enough' if you're active on social media. Social media can be good or bad, depending on how it is used. For example, it might feel easier talking over text since you're behind a screen, and you can take the time to filter out what you want to say before sending a message. You also feel a boost of confidence after getting some likes or compliments on your post uploads, and not to mention, the free, endless entertainment brought by memes and pet videos instantly brightens up a bad day. However, let's face the bitter reality of it as well.

Many social media users are willing to showcase only the 'picture-perfect', sunny parts of their lives. The people you follow online are most likely sharing only their best images. They share photos of the best times with their friends and family, what they had from the new expensive pop-up restaurant in town, and anything else that can paint a shade of glamour on their profile feeds. When you're a teenager, you're still developing an identity, and sometimes it feels easier to adopt the behaviour of others you want for yourself.

Other peoples' social media accounts are just selective highlights of their lives that they have carefully arranged to give themselves a good impression. Despite everyone having their fair share of struggles and shortcomings in life, they won't put that on display. It's easy to forget that no one's perfect. You're likely to fall into the trap of 'social comparison' at this time, where you compare yourself, your looks and your life to others and what they have going for them. Then comes the 'compare and despair' effect. You wish you could be more like others, especially if you aren't happy with who you are. Seeing others be more successful feels like you won't ever be good enough. But believe me, that could not be farther from the truth.

Some issues are deep and in your subconscious. You can't always trace the roots of those issues, let alone realise that they have been there this whole time. Learning about how the mind creates social anxiety will help you overcome it because you will have a name and face for what's giving you trouble. Once you have learned to identify it, it will get easier to face and overcome your fears because you will have gained the confidence to assert that you are fully capable, no matter the outcome, which is enough. You think you're alone, but you're not. Others are trying to find their way out of this dark land just like you. It's a human struggle and a shared experience that brings many of us together and connects us. Almost everyone experiences social anxiety to some degree, both teenagers and adults.

Social Anxiety is associated with chronic distress, fear and self-consciousness that sufferers experience to the point that it impairs them in social environments. This fear is a normal response to things we do not understand or have control over. It's there to protect us from dangerous situations. In the same way, pain lets you know you're hurt or injured, feeling fearful lets you know you're in potential danger. As Intelligent beings, we process information we gain from our surroundings. Therefore, we have the power to perceive our environment and choose how we respond to fear. Learning more about the fears you experience will give you the upper hand in the future. You will find that facing fear is a power that you can harness, which will help you with any problems you run into in the future.

It makes sense why you feel the way you do - you're scared. The grip that insecurities have on you can feel paralysing. But, while it seems impossible to see past your fears, that is precisely what you will learn to do.

Life is cool and fun on the other side of this brick wall of anxiety. You only need a ladder to climb it, which I will give you the tools to create, one step at a time. Envision yourself standing taller than the thoughts that belittle you, the fear of trying that holds you back, and the belief that "I am not good enough." Try seeing your remarkable self succeeding in everything you do. Imagine feeling, thinking or doing the opposite of all those situations described in the first few paragraphs of this introduction. Imagine waking up excited about your day ahead, feeling confident meeting people, being happy with yourself and who you are and having positive thoughts about your future. Sounds good, right? This is all possible.

Social anxiety is not a life sentence, but there are ways out, which I will help you map in this book. Overcoming fear means the weight of a whole scary world lifting off your shoulders. It is exhilarating. There are wonderful people out there to meet, and once you overcome social anxiety, you can meet and connect with them with so much freedom. Ah, freedom from fear. There are people you'll meet who will love and accept you for who you are. You only have to learn to let yourself have that. Your thoughts will be more complimentary and focused on the more positive and fun aspects of your life; with these thoughts, you'll feel better mentally AND physically. You'll walk taller with your head up and see, experience and appreciate much more than you do now.

There are skills to learn and little things you can start practising immediately to see significant changes. This book mentions and elaborates on several valuable techniques and strategies designed to help you improve your social skills, giving you perspective and helping you build faith in yourself. What you learn from this book will equip you with the tools you need to manage the anxiety you feel, help you learn more about yourself and help you cope with whatever life has in its hefty pockets to throw at you. You won't have to fear struggle because you'll have grown to trust yourself and the strength within you - a strength you have always had. This book explains why and how you feel and think the way you sometimes do, what that means and how it's affecting you. As well as tools to help you manage episodes of anxiety before, during and after the episodes, this book will also provide you with techniques to banish anxiety for good.

You will get better when you're willing to do the simple exercises which you are so capable of doing. A few gentle nudges or even a big shove, whatever it takes to get you to take the first step, then follow it with all the steps outlined in this book, and you'll start to feel and see dramatic changes in yourself and in your life.

I suffered from chronic anxiety throughout my childhood, which I carried into my adult life. It blocked me and held me back from the life I wanted for myself. I was determined to learn and push past these limitations because I knew deep down I deserved to have a life free to be myself. Social anxiety felt like a constant hurricane inside me which never seemed to relent. I couldn't live my life free to express myself and be me. I was always afraid of being laughed at and felt I was not good enough. Because I have been through these stresses, it breaks my heart to see others, especially teenagers, go through the same, feeling helpless as I did. You have your whole life ahead of you, and the sooner you nip this anxiety in the bud, the sooner you can take control of the life you were meant to lead. You do not have to take this into your adult years.

In this book, I have given you the tools and techniques I learned over the years to overcome anxiety once and for all. I have been a Chiropractor for 20 years and have been privileged to help people physically and mentally find relief from pain. I discovered that much of people's physical pain is directly linked to their mental state of mind, anxiety being one of the primary culprits. During this time of helping and serving others, I also worked extensively on myself to heal the anxiety. As a result, I grew stronger mentally, allowing me to help even more of my patients. I did years of self-improvement courses and read many books to understand why I felt the way I did. Here began the journey to becoming a Clinical Hypnotherapist and fully qualified and licensed Rapid Transformational Therapist (RTT). I love that I can continue to serve and help heal people quickly and with long-lasting results. You can check out my website at https://www.thashnawalsh.com to learn more. Enough about me though. This book is all about helping you.

I found the power to overcome my limitations, but what about the superpower like Professor X already within you? Well, you might not have the ability to control someone else's mind, but you certainly have the power to control your own mind, which is where your superpower lies. So, to begin this journey to an anxiety-free life, you first have to understand how your, and everyone's, mind works.

Super important

Before diving in, you will need a notebook or a journal dedicated to the exercises within this book. Preferably, start a fresh one and dedicate it to practising these different exercises and strategies to overcome social anxiety. It will never be enough to read any book and be changed forever. You must practice the exercises to get the changes coded and wired into your mind and body. Reading, writing, interacting and feeling together allow the changes to occur.

The first few chapters may feel a little sciency, but don't let that deter you. It's easy stuff, just follow along and understand the basics. This fundamental science is the foundation for your exercises which are the power tools for setting you free. You can read the book however you like. However, It is my advice that you understand Chapter 1 first. You will soon realise that this book is different to others you have read as it goes a little deeper to give you what you need. I understand as teenagers, the last thing you want is to be reading another book. However, if you use it well, this book is not just any other book but it will serve you for a long time. I believe in you; you have what it takes, and I will show you.

So, you say you are devoted to change? Get your pen, notebook/journal and your open mind and let's do this!

Chapter 1
How your mind works
Ways of the subconscious and conscious mind

> *Old ways won't open new doors*
>
> — Unknown

At rest, the brain uses up 20-25% of the body's total energy. That's more energy than any other organ in the body uses (Michaud 2015). So, concentrating or thinking about something requires a hell of a lot of energy. In addition, mental processes like making decisions and solving problems are hefty and consume a lot of mind power. So to save energy, the brain tries to develop ways to make other forms of thinking more manageable and efficient. One way is through splitting the brain into the conscious and subconscious mind.

To save energy and time, the brain also makes some processes automatic such as the fight-or-flight/fear response or most habits, behaviours and bodily functions. The subconscious mind controls these automated processes. However, the brain doesn't double-check subconscious processes and we never really think about that stuff, let alone notice it. It's like an inbuilt auto-pilot function once we learn it. For example, walking, riding a bike, or automatically scrolling on social media.

Freud's model of the mind mentions that most of our mind's work is done by the unconscious mind, i.e., the subconscious (Sousa 2011). The subconscious mind also attaches meaning and emotion to memories and experiences. It can help you learn whether to seek out or avoid certain experiences in the future. Hence, it helps us quickly develop a positive or negative attitude toward something.

There's a difference between the brain processing information and you experiencing that processing. The processing of logic, creative thought, rational and analytical thinking is done by your conscious mind, which is 5% of your mind (See Diagram 1). Currently, you are aware that you're reading this page of a book and making sense of it logically. At the same time, you are aware of the surface you're sitting on, the sounds around you, if it's light or dark outside, and so on. However, the conscious mind is aware of limited information at a time and only of what's happening in real time.

Your subconscious mind is a constantly expanding universe that records and replays what it learns. It controls 95% of your brain's function (See Diagram 1). Everything happening around you is fed into it and shapes your belief and how you see and rationalise the world based on those experiences. The meaning you give to your experiences is stored in the subconscious mind to be easily accessed in the future when similar experiences occur. It is where you pull up beliefs about what it meant when you felt ignored or forgotten or when you said 'hello' to a group of classmates and didn't get a reply. You may believe they don't like you because you are not cool or pretty enough.

These beliefs limit you because you allow them to make you feel less of who you truly are. Think about it, who were you before you ever experienced thinking negatively about yourself? Your subconscious stores limiting beliefs (beliefs not aligned with the facts, such as phobias which limit you). Your subconscious also stores healthy non-limiting beliefs such as; "I am pretty awesome, and everyone loves me". Your subconscious responds to what you tell yourself, good or bad; it cannot analyse and reason like your conscious mind.

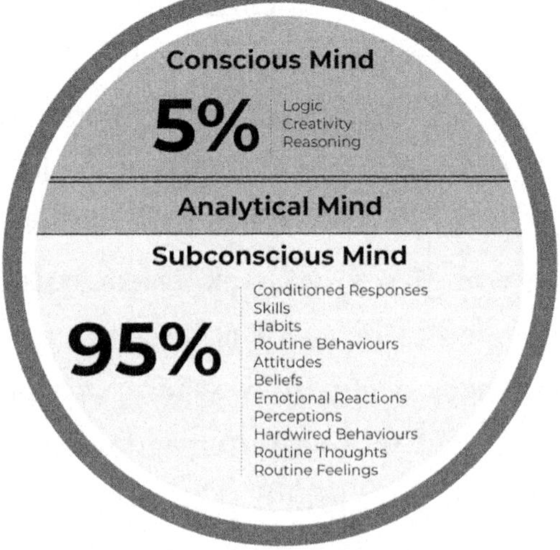

Diagram 1: *The Mind: Conscious and Subconscious: Adapted from Dr Joe Dispenza's model of the mind*

Say you had a horrible experience as a young child, such as the kids in school didn't want to play with you because you looked different. Unless an intuitive adult helped you to make sense of what was happening, you would create your own analysis. Young children almost always blame themselves, so you may think something is wrong with you, you are not enough, unlovable, and so on. The analysis over time is accepted by the subconscious mind and stored. As a teenager, you still have these subconscious beliefs stored, fuelling social anxiety, so you don't speak to other students in school because you think they won't want to hang out with you. Get the picture? See how your subconscious mind is trying to help you in this situation by replaying the stored recording from years ago when you were a child. In this case, it is clearly not helping though, is it?

Your subconscious does not think; it is merely replaying a recorded or programmed response that helped you through an ordeal in the past. Once you 'survive' an ordeal, you will automatically save this memory in your mind so you can 'survive' any similar ordeal in the future by quickly retrieving this stored memory without reflection or analysis to help you make quick 'survival' decisions. The subconscious holds a vast set of practised or imprinted memories stored for present and future reference to help make your life easier (Dispenza 2007). The question is, what are you practising and imprinting on your subconscious that will automatically pop up to 'help' you later? Are you putting yourself down, or are you feeling not good enough? Where is your focus 95% of the day? Being aware of this makes you aware of what is being programmed in your mind and continues to be programmed until you change your focus.

There is hope though. When you feel that you are unhappy, that you are stuck and wish you could change, or that you cannot break a habit that is neither benefiting you nor letting you live the genuine, fun and happy life that you want, that's a clue; you are aware that your subconscious beliefs are no longer serving you. You have grown past them, and it's time to change them. Here is where you start breaking bad habits, harmful thinking patterns and letting go of limiting beliefs. Isn't it exciting? You won't be like this forever.

What you believe, is your experience

Let's have a look at how the way you think, feel, and as a result, what you believe affects the life you live. What does your mind resort to when something doesn't work out in your favour? Do you feel bad about yourself? Do you put yourself down and lose faith in yourself and your abilities, or do you blame others or something for how YOU think and feel and give up? Or do you pick yourself up and try again and again until you succeed? Do you believe failure is a lesson or the end? Imagine choosing to believe in yourself as confident, capable, and totally awesome. What you believe will be your experience. The negative belief will bring negativity. Positive beliefs will bring a positive and happy life. So, how do you believe 'right' for the outcome you want?

You were not born with social anxiety; no one was. Look at a baby; they are confident as can be; they let you know when they are happy or unhappy regardless of where they are and who's watching. As they grew up, they got conditioned to think in a certain way and have particular beliefs based on the environment they were born and raised in. We are all outcomes of the conditioning we have experienced as children, from our parents, caregivers, teachers and friends. So, essentially, your beliefs are shaped by the world and people around you, which have shaped the behaviours and thoughts that you have now.

If the mind is programmed and conditioned to be the way it is, it can also be reconditioned. You can reprogram your mind to live a confident, happier, more fulfilling life. It can take days to weeks to reprogram your subconscious mind; it only depends on how deeply ingrained your habits and beliefs you'd like to change are (Bargh 2008), the techniques used, and the determination to make it happen.

'Reprogramming' your mind may sound weird and like something you do to computers, but really, it's just a way to change how you think with consistent practice of some self-help approaches that we'll have a look at soon.

You can consciously decide to be more productive, more outgoing, and less of a hermit and then do it. However, to do this consistently when your subconscious program is set to do the opposite will be next to impossible. This is because your subconscious beliefs control 95% of your life, and your subconscious mind's job is to keep you alive and surviving using the programs you installed in it at an earlier time. It will not allow you to change its programming so easily, especially not after it's been working 'so well' for so long. So, your 5% conscious mind must be unrelenting to overcome. How often have you tried to start studying, for example, and found yourself repeatedly distracted? This subconscious interruption is because studying for you may not be fun. If studying was not programmed as fun in your subconscious but was programmed as pain. Your subconscious will recall the program that protects you from pain. So it distracts you with other pleasurable things, such as games or social media, etc. Do you see the paradox? How can you get good grades when your subconscious mind seems to be sabotaging you?

It sounds a little unfair. Why can't you change for the better when you want to? Why does the mind that is meant to keep you feeling safe, limit and hold you back from being free to be your best self? Do you know what I mean? For example, you're scared of failing, but you can't study, you are scared of being humiliated, rejected, or ignored, so your mind shuts you down to avoid situations to keep you safe. What about having a perfectionist attitude where you are scared that it will not be perfect, so you decide not to try to save face? Maybe you become overwhelmed by something, and if you complete it, it will help you achieve your goal, but you are afraid of the unknown. After all, you could embarrass/hurt yourself, so your subconscious mind in all its wisdom distracts you or creates excuses for you to avoid the situation to protect you from potential physical or emotional harm. You must learn to bring awareness/consciousness to these subconscious replays and update them.

The Monkey Mind

There's a term called 'The Monkey Mind'. It describes a way of being. Imagine a monkey jumping from one tree to another, grabbing for food wherever it finds it; it's constantly on the move. The monkey mind wants what it wants when it wants. It uses a lot of energy and has a lot of cravings responding to multiple streams of thought. It's constantly thinking of everything it must do instead of what it's doing now. It's a stressful, overstimulated state. It leads to anxiety and doesn't allow you to focus on the bigger picture, here in the moment. The Monkey Mind is a state of hyper-sensitivity. Your behaviour is controlled by the emotional responses of the subconscious mind instead of the conscious mind that focuses on rational thinking or the logic behind things. We all have this monkey mind which is a part of our primal instincts. The primary function of the monkey mind is survival. It feeds the subconscious to generate fear in uncertainty to avoid unfamiliar, difficult or dangerous situations or thoughts that it may not feel comfortable confronting. It seeks out the danger and focuses on negative worst-case scenarios, so it's always ready to run away or fight if necessary. This chronic anxious worry may have served our cave-dwelling ancestors, but it does not help us in today's world. It can make it impossible for us to work under pressure, interact with each other in a healthy manner and deal with our fears appropriately. You can observe this monkey mind of yours and tame it.

Knocking at the door of your subconscious mind saying - "Hey, I don't want to feel this anxiety, calm down, be rational, can we please change?"- will not work as I explained earlier. Regardless of how hard you try to grasp your conscious tools to force change, it will not be enough, unless you have incredible willpower. Your subconscious mind wants to keep you safe, and despite the discomfort you feel when you are fearful, it is doing its best to ensure you survive, often at the expense of your happiness. Therefore, you must access the program controlled by the subconscious mind and tame the monkey mind at its root - All our limitations lie in the subconscious program. Social Anxiety is no exception. To get to the unwanted subconscious program, you must first understand what it is.

How do I really feel about things?

Allow me to guide you through an exercise that will help you reflect on your thoughts and feelings. After all, self-reflection is the best way to spend time getting to know your subconscious programming and learning to make peace with your mind. Have your notebook or journal ready to write down your thoughts on this exercise and all the other exercises in this book.

This exercise in particular, will help you address some of the thoughts you have and things you do that do not make any rational sense, but you feel stuck with them. For example, when you find yourself in a scenario where the voices of uncertainty and self-doubt are so loud inside your head, you're forced to look for ways out. How do you feel about yourself then? Pen and notebook/journal ready?

You will map out what's called a "thinking cycle." Think of a social scenario or a time when you felt so strongly that it made you feel fearful and anxious.

Exercise 1: What if?

Imagine you're at a club meeting and you usually get the seat closest to the back of the room to avoid attention. The head of the club starts by asking for everyone's feedback. He scans the room, and his eyes fall on you. He points to you and asks, "Hey, what are your thoughts?"

What do you think at that time? What is it that you feel? How do you act? Do you speak up and share what you have to say? Can you even think at that moment? Can you think of what might happen after, and why? What could you have done differently? How do you see the situation playing out differently, and what thoughts do you have about yourself then?

When you have given yourself a scenario, answer these questions sincerely:

- What did I think (THOUGHT)?
- How did I feel (FEELING)?
- How did I respond (ACTION) to what I felt?
- Did I believe I could respond adequately (BELIEF)
- Was the way that I responded helpful (BELIEF)? Or did it make me feel worse (BELIEF)?
- What did I expect, and did I achieve my desired outcome?

Once you have answered these questions and you have a picture of how you think and feel. You will also be able to see how you see yourself. Perhaps you believe that you aren't a confident person and that others think of you the same way. Pause and challenge that belief with a "what if?"

What if you ARE confident? What if you CAN speak up and others DO value what you have to say?

Dedicate some time to sitting down with your thoughts and doing this exercise and challenging any negative ideas. You are preparing to be mindful in the future, so that when you do end up on the spot, you remember your exercise and how you addressed any worries.

> *We cannot solve our problems with the same thinking we used to create them*
>
> — Albert Einstein

Exercise 2: Praise Time

Give yourself some credit. Remind yourself of instances where you were successful and confident in the past.

Remember the little and the big victories, and you will have proof and reason to believe in yourself.

In your journal, list 10 or more things you consider to be victories about yourself.

It's all about the vibes

When you think of something consciously, that thought will signal your unconscious brain saying, "Hey, how do we feel about this?" The feeling or emotion that pops up will drive you to carry out a particular action or a series of actions. The purpose of that is to achieve the desired outcome. When the outcome matches your thought, that thought will be confirmed as true. It goes: thought > feeling > action > outcome > affirmed thought i.e. a belief. It becomes a cycle. This cycle feeds your subconscious mind.

When another thought of similar charge, frequency, and energy is generated, the cycle continues deepening the belief. This continues until something shocks you into breaking that cycle, or you get into your subconscious mind to confront the feelings holding you back and change the belief.

Diagram 2: *The Thinking Cycle: Adapted from the book: Confidence Reload by Dr Thashna Walsh*

Social anxiety is a thought cycle that makes up a belief, and so is a lack of social anxiety. What will it take to break this negative thought cycle for you?

Belief in something must be more than a thought; it has to be a part of you, the experience of the thought, your emotions, and your actions. So, if you want to believe, but your actions do not match up, it is because you do not believe it at your core, subconscious level. Like I talked about studying earlier, you are distracted because your program/belief is different to your wish. Similarly, a program in your brain has developed a resistance to having confidence and high self-esteem. A program called 'social anxiety.'

We're going to get a little 'sciencey' now. Some elementary discussion of science will be relevant here because it relates to how your beliefs, behaviours, and habits interact. If you've covered the topic of electromagnetic energy in physics class, you'll most likely find this quite fascinating.

Energy makes up all the nature of things around us, including ourselves. So let's look at things for the following few paragraphs from the point of view of energy whilst remembering that thoughts create feelings and emotions, which themselves are energy.

Your energy can be measured using Kinesiology and a set of parameters of consciousness measuring from 10 to 1000. Take a look at the Map of Consciousness in Diagram 3. Where are you right about now based on how you are feeling? Most of the human consciousness today is tossing back and forth between 10 to 200.

A lack of confidence will put you in the zone of anxiety, which is noted at 100 on the map. Maintaining this frequency can only pull you further down the scale in time. Aiming to sustain your vibrations about and above the 200 mark will make you strong and confident on so many levels, which will inspire, illuminate and transform not only you but those around you as well.

Map of Consciousness

A limited set of parameters of consciousness calibrated from 1-1000 (logarithm to the base 10) of the power of the respective fields. From book by David Hawkins, Power vs Force

	GOD-VIEW	LIFE-VIEW	LEVEL	SCALE	EMOTION	PROCESS
POWER/ STRONG	Self	Is	Enlightenment	700-1000	Ineffable	Pure Consciousness
	All Being	Perfect	Peace	600	Bliss	Illumination
	One	Complete	Joy	540	Serenity	Transfiguration
	Loving	Benign	Love	500	Reverence	Revelation
	Wise	Meaningful	Reason	400	Understanding	Abstraction
	Merciful	Harmonious	Acceptance	350	Forgiveness	Transcendence
	Inspiring	Hopeful	Willingness	310	Optimism	Intention
	Enabling	Satisfactory	Neutrality	250	Trust	Release
	Permitting	Feasible	Courage	200	Affirmation	Empowerment
FORCE/ WEAK	Indifferent	Demanding	Pride	175	Scorn	Aggression
	Vengeful	Antagonistic	Anger	150	Hate	Inflation
	Denying	Dissapointing	Desire	125	Craving	Enslavement
	Punitive	Frightening	Fear	100	Anxiety	Withdrawal
	Distainful	Tragic	Grief	75	Regret	Despondency
	Condemning	Hopeless	Apathy	50	Dispair	Abdication
	Vindictive	Evil	Guilt	30	Blame	Destruction
	Despising	Miserable	Shame	20	Humiliation	Elimination

***Diagram** 3: Map of Consciousness: Adapted from Professor David Hawkins' book Power vs Force.*

Spend a little time studying this and understand why you may have an anxiety issue. Anxiety calibrates in the fear zone of 100. Confidence calibrates in the courage zone of 200. So can you see why you need to change your energy?

The real challenge is committing yourself to the habits that will help you rewire your subconscious mind and raise your vibrations to an energy level that charges your confidence.

Once you have reached a higher energy level, the work will not entirely end there. You want to protect it from your own negative energy (thoughts) and that of others. It's pretty easy if you remember not to be so hard on yourself. You can uplift yourself by complimenting yourself, accepting compliments from others, and practising positive affirmations like telling yourself that you deserve to feel safe with your thoughts and that you deserve good things in life as much as anyone else does. Safe-keep your positive energy by looking for the good in every situation and practising gratitude. Shift your focus to what you feel good about and the good that can potentially happen, rather than what feels scary or wrong about a situation.

Sit down with your journal. Spend some time thinking about "your best self."

Your Best Self is someone you wish to be. To be your best self, you will need to reflect on your character, your strengths, what you're good at (even the smallest of things), what you can do to help others, and why you think that version of you is your best. Our lives are built on the stories we tell ourselves. So, try telling yourself better stories, your best stories. Here is a little hint: your best self is already there in you. It's only buried under negativity and fears, so get digging and find yourself underneath all the false beliefs. Dig deep.

Exercise 3: Tell your best self-story

Think about a time you felt accomplished, optimistic, energised, and pleased about yourself, so much that you

couldn't wait to get home and tell everyone how well you did.

Maybe you got an A on your midterm, won a prize, perhaps cooked something at home that everyone loved so much, or you made someone's day by complimenting them. The minor things also count because they still make you feel good for a while, no matter how small. So you want to focus on your happy self and be empowered by it.

Now, write about that time. Your story will have a start, a middle, and a strong ending. Write in as much detail as possible and highlight your strengths, thoughts, and most importantly, the feelings you felt during that time. Get creative and use as much description as you can. Use all your senses (what you see, hear, feel, smell and taste) to describe who you are, what you are doing, why you are doing it, how you feel, and why you feel this way. Hear what people around you are saying and what you are saying to yourself.

- What was happening?
- What actions did you take to help yourself or someone else?
- How did you feel? Before, during, and after?

After writing the story, read it back to yourself while imagining stepping into this personality as your best self.

What would your best self say to you to encourage you?

Write down a positive, empowering statement you can say to yourself to remind yourself of your strengths and abilities.

In addition to the actions you took, expand on the list.

What can I do better next time? What other actions would help me feel more confident?

Ask yourself, "What new energy level do you want to choose for yourself?" followed by, "what will you do to get there?"

Write down how you feel in yourself after the exercise, what's your energy like now?

Wouldn't you like to have courage so you can have the strength inside you to work toward your goals, feel good about yourself, and look forward to most days rather than dreading them? You can opt to follow the empowerment process to feel more affirmed in life at the measure of 200 on the scale and start working from there. What can you do to empower yourself? You can begin by speaking kinder to yourself, having positive self-talk, and even celebrating the little victories like waking up on time in the morning and making your bed.

So, what will it be? The courage to change and walk where the grass is greener? Or withdrawal from life and giving in to worry and anxiety forever?

Let's move on and explore ways to tap into your energy levels and bring them up so that you radiate only 'positive vibes'. For example, you can always tell that a person is confident and has healthy self-esteem because they speak with a positive outlook on life. They give off positive energy, attracting others to their high vibes. That is why confidence is attractive. People like being around people that love themselves enough to be genuine and open. It helps others learn to appreciate themselves too.

You will also learn how you have unconsciously attracted the life you currently have and how you can consciously change your energy to support and give you a new life full of the confidence you want and much more.

Everything gives off unique energy, and you interact with your environment based on energy via your thoughts and feelings. All things vibrate to give off a particular frequency of energy. All shapes, sounds, smells, and tastes feel different depending on the differences in their vibrations. Even the air is filled with particles vibrating at different energy frequencies. Everything in the universe is in motion; we don't realise it because we can't always see the vibrations. For example, every object you can see vibrates at a frequency visible to human eyes. The range of frequency visible to the human eye is extremely low compared to what's around us, which means that the objects we're able to see are vibrating very slowly, and that's why our eyes can see them in their physical form. So, only a tiny fraction of the electromagnetic energy that surrounds us (the visible spectrum) is detectable by the human eye, but there is lots more going on around us that we cannot see, such as radio waves, UV rays, microwaves, etc.

The Quantum Atom

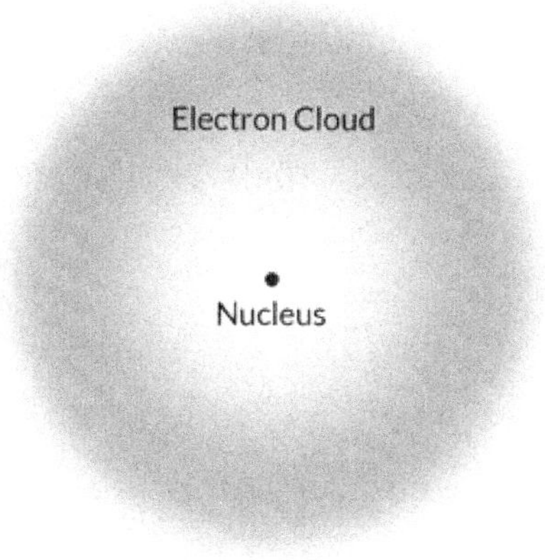

Diagram 4: *The Quantum Atom: Adapted from the book by Dr. Joe Dispenza: Breaking the Habit of Being Yourself.*

Another way to look at this energy we are so integrated with is to go back to the common factor within all things living and non-living. Everything is made up of atoms. The atom comprises 99.99999 percent energy and 0.00001 percent matter (physical things).

The quantum version of the atom with an electron cloud. The atom is 99.99999 percent energy and .00001 matter. Its almost nothing materially

What does this mean? It means that, because you are an accumulation of atomic particles, you are 99.99999 percent 'energy', and the rest of you is 'matter', so you are no different from everything else in the known universe, which is vibrating at different frequencies to make up real life.

Your physical body is a tiny 0.00001%. And, though you can't see it, your energy field (99.9999%) is about 9 feet (3 metres) wide and surrounds you and interacts with the energy field of everyone around you, as their energy field interacts with yours.

We tend to only focus on the tiny 'matter' (physical) parts of ourselves because we can see, touch, taste, smell, and hear these. However, we are mostly unaware of the vast potential we have to create and shape things with our extraordinary minds by changing our 'energy' for positive outcomes in our lives. That, of course, includes your self-esteem and confidence. When you put yourself under a lot of undue stress such as anxiety, you drain your energy field, as you have learned by looking at the Map of consciousness (See Diagram 3). So how can you tap into your energy to free yourself from anxiety, nurture self-esteem and confidence and manifest good things in your life? By being conscious of how you think, the foods you eat, the company you keep, the environment where you spend your time, and so on. We will get to this; however, let's help you understand more about anxiety, what it is and some of the different types.

Chapter 2
The many faces of anxiety
What is anxiety

> *If it doesn't challenge you, it won't change you.*
>
> — Thashna Walsh

S*ay it, come on. Say it, now's the time!*

But you can't. You're being crushed under the weight of wanting to say the right thing at the right time, but you are thinking, what if I am misunderstood? What if I make a fool of myself? What if I stutter? What if I get ignored or laughed at? These 'what if' thoughts you have outside of the present moment paralyse you moving forward because they are based in a time that has not happened yet, the future, so, there is nothing you can do about it. Hence the anxiety. After all, you cannot fix something that does not exist. What can you fix then? You can only fix what is happening in the present moment, which, right now is nothing to fear, because you are safe where you are right at this very moment, reading this book. What else can you fix? If your thoughts create your emotions and your emotions create your energy, why not change the thinking to something else?

Anxiety is the inability to turn your brain off from thinking inefficiently by tagging all incoming thoughts with faults or warning signs. It's the inability to stop painting a negative picture of every possible thought, reaction or action. In other words, it's the failure to choose healthy thoughts to focus on. Instead, you focus on the negative ones.

"They're annoyed with me". "Things won't work out". "No one likes me". "I'm never going to be good at anything".

Your brain creates problems that don't exist. It's your thoughts telling your body you are in danger when there is no danger.

The way your body functions is directly related to your thoughts and emotions. You know that feeling of dread you get in your chest for a split second when you think, "OMG, I'm gonna fall" because you missed a step on the stairs, but you didn't. After a few moments, you composed yourself and got on with life, no sweat, all forgotten. Anxiety causes the same symptoms, except that feeling stays in your chest for hours and days on end. Nothing may be wrong, but you think and feel everything is, using up so much energy, leaving you drained and your body tired and exposed to illness.

This sustained anxiousness manifests physically in ways such as stomach indigestion, heart palpitations, feeling queasy or nauseated, muscle pains or tension typically in the back, neck, and shoulders due to being on edge all the time, headaches, sensitivity to light and sounds, and much more. These symptoms all start with chronic negative thoughts.

When I said "hello" to XYZ, "did I sound rude?" "They didn't respond to me; did I do something wrong?" "They don't like me". "Whatever, screw them". "Hang on, that's not fair". "What if they didn't hear me?" "What if they're having a bad day?"

Anxiety is caused by the constant questioning of everything you say and do. It's a program that auto-runs as you go over everything you said or heard in a day, all the ways in which you acted or how others acted towards you. You have lost the present moment, living in the future you have created in your mind based on the worst that could happen. It isn't only a feeling of passing nervousness but when the stress response is out of control. Anxiety is also a mental health disorder when it affects your ability to live life as you want to. It has psychological symptoms and can also appear physically in chronic states.

Some people believe it is good to have a level of worry and anxiety to demonstrate they care about others, but this is flawed thinking. Of course, having a healthy awareness of each other is important. However, when the hormones of stress (cortisol and adrenaline) rise in the bloodstream, this is the time to fight, flee or freeze; it's not a time for nurturing. Besides, in the long run, these hormones in your bloodstream cause physical damage to your body. I will talk about the fight, flee, or freeze response in more detail soon.

On the other hand, when you are calm and focused on positive thoughts, you see the world with clear and controlled eyes; your body is in homeostasis, and you feel safe and able to contribute positively to yourselves and others. That said, most people live with a certain amount of anxiety which they manage in various ways. Some people don't even realise they are anxious and believe it's their personality and therefore can't be changed. Others may use modalities such as yoga, meditation, breathing techniques, mindfulness, music, food, drugs, and alcohol. Some of these modalities, such as comfort eating, drugs and alcohol, may not necessarily be the healthiest solution but give temporary relief.

Your mind does not know the difference between something happening in real life and something that is imagined with lots of emotions. So, though anxiety is based on the thought of something that has not happened for real but is imagined, it is still felt with the same intensity as if it's real, and the body responds accordingly. Anxiety is the mind's way of telling your body that something is up, and it needs to act immediately, remember? Racing heart, sweating, nausea and dizziness, your mind is hyper-alert, headaches, and feeling weak in the arms and legs.

While it is true that not all anxiety is the same as an anxiety disorder, anxiety that makes your life difficult overall is a problem.

What fuels social anxiety?

The thoughts and ideas of yourself that you are not good enough or you're going to look like a fool cause you to act out of fear, such as fear of being judged or disappointing others. You carry out behaviours like staying home, cancelling plans, avoiding being seen by people or being around them; whatever ways you can to prevent those fears. Behaviours like this can help you feel safe short-term if there is a real threat. However, this is an unconscious response. This fearful response to your thoughts keeps the social anxiety alive and stops you from evolving through your life. The world is highly stimulating. There is always so much going on, and it's not easy for young minds to take it all in and also figure out what's going on with themselves. The news is often alarming, leaving people questioning what else might be written for them in the future and whether it will get worse or better. This uncertainty of the future typically fuels anxiety of any form.

Early traumatic experiences can also predispose someone to anxiety. In addition, environmental factors such as your upbringing, experience of home when you were little, parents, guardians, teachers, peers, and lifestyle are other factors to consider when managing any form of anxiety, as they all fuel this state.

For better chances at survival, human beings have evolved and adopted ways to help protect themselves from threats or danger. There is an instinctive response within us called the 'fight, flight or freeze' or the stress response, activated by anything the brain perceives as a threat. When the brain thinks you're in danger, the sympathetic nervous system, a network of nerves carrying information to different organs and glands all over the body, is activated. It activates the hypothalamus in the brain, sending signals to the adrenal medulla to release the hormones adrenaline and cortisol. When these hormones are released into your bloodstream, your heart pounds faster, and blood rushes to your hands and feet; you start to sweat and breathe faster, so you are ready to run and do what it takes to survive. You also focus on what is causing the threat and make a memory in your subconscious mind for future reference. These hormones are harmless and very useful in real and acutely stressful situations for short periods to get you out of danger and to safety. Once the threat subsides, the body regulates, and the hormone levels return to normal. However, suppose you dwell on the stressful situation, playing it over and over in your mind, feeling the emotions of stress. In that case, the stress hormones remain at high levels in your bloodstream as your subconscious feels you are still under threat, making you chronically anxious. So you see, anxiety occurs whether the threat is real or imagined. The point is, you believe it is real.

The same happens when you overthink why you can't stand and present something to the class, go to that party or speak up for yourself. Your response to protecting yourself is to avoid the potential situation because you feel as if you can't think or talk, your muscles stiffen, so it feels harder to move, and you may even start to feel sick to avoid doing these things. Though this is ideal when you want to hide away from your assignment or social engagement, what are you hiding from though? "I don't want to hide"; you may even think to yourself. Then why is it all so hard not to? You know you cannot be running away from life and its challenges all the time. The situations that trigger you will not cease, and you cannot outrun them because they're a part of life. When this instinctual, subconscious part of your brain is overstimulated, it blocks your brain's intelligent, conscious part from functioning. So, of course, you can't hold an intelligent conversation, and how you want to behave will be hindered until you recognise your faulty thinking and rewire your subconscious mind.

It is therefore essential to note that your body is regulating the stress efficiently; however, your thoughts reliving the stressful situation repeatedly perpetuate the anxiety. Your mind does what you tell it. So if you keep worrying and emotionalising about the potential of something terrible happening, your mind thinks it is real and stimulates the body to respond accordingly. Let's go into this a little deeper.

Types of Anxiety

There are different types of anxiety. Knowing about some of them can help you understand the anxiety you or someone else may be experiencing and better understand how to manage it effectively with some exercises.

Anxiety in its general form evolves when a person focuses on thoughts the body interprets as harmful which can cause hurt and limit their abilities. The different types of anxiety vary in their intensity. For example, the feeling of tingling in your fingers and butterflies in your stomach before presenting to the class is different from the sickly sense of impending doom you might feel in your chest doing something as simple as crossing the road. Here are some types of anxiety to consider their differences and similarities.

Anticipatory anxiety

This type of anxiety relates to the feelings of fear or worry that you might experience before an event, such as a date, party, public speaking event, job interview, or performance. It can also occur in going about routine everyday tasks and occurrences such as walking to school or going out to eat. This kind of anxiety pulls your focus toward adverse outcomes and thoughts about everything that could go wrong, the worst-case scenarios and all the what if's, no matter how unlikely. This form of anxiety, like all others, is irrational.

It is not so much a mental health condition as a symptom of anxiety disorders. So, here's an exercise you can practise to deal with anticipatory anxiety.

Exercise 4: Guide your imagination

Imagine yourself doing exceptionally well when you thought you couldn't. Imagine everything working out in your favour and going smoothly the way you planned.

Sit in a comfortable place and breathe slowly, in a calculated way. Take a deep breath in through the nose and out through the mouth.

Let's visualise you walking into class on your first day of school. It took you a while to find your classroom, but you're there. You stand at the door. You can hear everyone talking inside, and you start feeling butterflies in your chest and stomach. You get a little tense, but it's okay. These sensations are perfectly normal. You don't need to shoo them away.

How does it feel to feel emotions without trying to escape them? It's okay if you feel uncomfortable. Cross your arms over your chest and hug yourself to self-

soothe. Take a deep breath and become present with your body.

Think to yourself: "I can handle this feeling. It's not here to hurt me. I'm always safe as long as I am present with myself."

You step into the class and notice all the new faces. Some people turn to look at who walked in, and they see you. You see them too. You're scared again ("What are they thinking about me? Do I look weird?"). They're too busy thinking about themselves to stop and turn their attention to you. Now you remember that you're safe and you can handle this feeling, as it's not to hurt you.

Remember to keep breathing slow and deep throughout this imagery.

After walking into class, you shift your attention to what else is around you. The clock on the wall, the colours of the posters on the notice board, how clean the floor is (or isn't), how you like this one girl's sneakers, and finally, the empty seat at the back. You quickly reach the empty chair and put your backpack down. No one's looking at you anymore; everyone's busy talking.

You now start to worry that no one wants to be your friend. You notice this thought, and it pains you.

Pause. Take a moment to feel this out.

These thoughts don't speak the truth. You aren't a bad person. Of course you want to be a good friend. There are people that like what you like. You have many jokes and favourite stories to share with others. You're especially great at noticing what others need. You're just in a new place. Take time to feel comfortable with yourself being around others.

The anxiety is still there. It's okay, feel it, smile at yourself for wanting to protect yourself and keep breathing deeply, knowing you are safe. Remember, it's a new situation, and everyone has to go through it; you only need to give it a little time.

Class has started and everyone has settled down. It's your favourite subject, English. The teacher walks in and introduces herself; she seems nice. This lesson will be on creative writing, and you are excited. You are starting to feel better already.

The anxiety is still there, but it's quieter now because you acknowledged it. Instead of pushing it away, you became comfortable with the uncomfortable. So now the discomfort is pretty much gone.

Time passes, and class is over; you start getting ready to leave when someone comes to your desk. It's the girl whose shoes you liked. She says hi and smiles at you. You were scared that no one would want to be your friend, but

here someone is saying hello to you first. You say hi back, and she sits down next to you. This is your moment.

You tell her that you like her shoes and it makes her really happy. The two of you leave class and walk home together while talking and getting to know each other.

So, this will be a reminder that your negative anticipation did not match up with what the reality was. You felt a lot of discomforts today, but you allowed yourself to experience it and let it pass over you instead of letting it affect you.

You're paving a path of emotional growth and strength, and it's pretty cool. Keep up the great work.

The next time you're afraid of things going wrong or being embarrassed, think back to this exercise and create a positive guided imagery for yourself. If you can get through it once in your head, you can also get through it in real life. The gross majority of the negative things you worry about will never happen.

The key point here is to practice mindfulness to help you be more in tune with how you feel about your surroundings and learn to look at things differently.

The anxiety reappraisal technique (Exercise 15, Chapter 7) will also help you reframe your perspective and re-adjust how you interpret your feelings. So instead of calling your feelings anxiety, nervousness or saying that you are worried, shift your mindset. For instance, instead of saying, "I feel anxious," go with, "I'm excited!" or "I'm looking forward to how things turn out." See chapter 7 for more on this.

Did you know that when you experience fear or excitement, the hormones released in your body are practically the same? The only reason you feel different is the perception you give to the experience. Your thoughts create your feelings, and your feelings create your action, which creates your outcome. So use this exercise to assess your thoughts and create different, more optimistic, compelling thoughts for better outcomes.

Generalised Anxiety Disorder, also referred to as GAD or free-floating anxiety

GAD is a chronic and inflated sense of worry that occurs spontaneously, without a source to pin it on. People with this type of anxiety spend much of their time worrying about a broader range of future events and matters. The anxiety they experience tends to centre on their health, work, relationships, social encounters, and events that are as far as months into the future or as close as the next few hours.

In cases where such excessive worrying interferes with the person's essential areas of life, and they feel it most days, lasting longer than six months, they must be recommended to see a healthcare provider or mental health professional.

Some symptoms of GAD include: problems coping with uncertainty, difficulty concentrating, an inability to stop racing, worrying thoughts, constantly feeling on edge, being quick to think of the worst possible outcome in any situation, and having more excessive worries than the actual problem.

Panic

Panic is a more severe and sudden type of anxiety. When a person experiences a panic attack, it can be disabling. It is characterised by a sense of impending doom, feeling out of control or as if one is dying, sweating, cold or pinprick sensations in the hands and feet, and racing heart or chest pain. Panic attacks occur out of the blue and don't always have a specific trigger. They are a symptom of an anxiety disorder called panic disorder. People that struggle with panic disorder worry that they'll experience a panic attack, so they avoid situations and places where they suspect an attack may occur.

Deep breathing is helpful. There is more about breathing in chapter 6. The grounding technique also proves very beneficial. When you're having an anxiety or panic attack, your mind is racing too fast, and the fight, flight or freeze response gets overstimulated. Grounding techniques can help reel you back into reality and remind you that you're safe. Grounding focuses you back to where you are in the present and what's around you.

Grounding is simple. You use any or all five of your senses to calm down and distract your mind from its panic.

Practice doing these techniques till you're sure you can remember to use them the next time you're in distress.

Exercise 5: Grounding technique

A. Do maths or use numbers:

- **Pick a number and think of 3 ways to make it e.g. 4 (2 x 2 = 4, 2 + 2 = 4, 10 - 6 = 4)**
- **Pick a times table in your head and go through it.**

B. Name items from broad categories:

Choose from a mental list of broad categories, and take a minute or two to name all you can.

- **Stationery supplies**
- **Kitchen items**
- **Musical instruments**
- **The apps on your phone**
- **Languages**
- **And so on.**

C. Visualise:

Imagine walking away from the pain you are feeling. You can imagine shutting your negative emotions and overflowing thoughts into one big suitcase and kicking it off the end of a cliff. You can also think that you have a dial on your thoughts that you can use to turn their volume down.

Describe what's around you

Pick up any object and say 3 things about it.

- "This cup is plastic; it is red and empty."
- "This key is made of metal, it is shiny, and it jingles."
- "This chair is cushioned, it is made of wood, and it's painted brown."

D. Practice kindness and compassion toward yourself

Repeat the following to yourself as many times as you need, either out loud or in your heart:

- "I'm feeling uncomfortable, but I can make it through."
- "I'm doing my best right now, and it is enough."
- "This challenging time will not last. I will come out the other side just fine."

Performance anxiety

More commonly known as stage fright, this type of anxiety is related to a person's ability to carry out a specific task when expected to, such as giving a presentation, auditioning for a play, doing a test or competing in a sporting event.

Feeling a little fear is natural when facing the unknown world of performing. The fight, flight or freeze response from this kind of stress makes your body more alert, preparing you to handle the situation mentally and physically. Use it! However, if this fear exceeds a certain point, it becomes anxiety, it can hinder performance and make it rather difficult for you to perform well. So, you may forget important details and start getting distracted as your mind feels like it's going numb or that all your thoughts are scrambled or replaced by static.

Phobias

A phobia is an intense fear of a particular object or situation. Examples of phobias include a fear of heights, snakes, needles or the sight of blood. People experience anxiety regarding their phobias because they worry about encountering the source of their fear. As a result, they'll go to lengths to avoid the object of their fear. For example, a person that has a fear of seeing blood might avoid getting their medical tests done or avoid going to the hospital at all.

Avoidance is a coping strategy common in those with social phobias such as social anxiety. You have probably felt intensely hopeless when doing something that scares you. This avoidance can be pretty obvious such as not going to places you've been invited to, not replying to texts, and staying inside all the time. You may even demonstrate this by; avoiding eye contact, not taking the same path on a walk everyone else is taking, choosing to keep your distance from others, not smiling back at others and avoiding small talk.

The exposure technique has been a successful tool to help decrease avoidant behaviour and increase your chances to rise above the fears. It focuses on changing your behaviour by exposing you to the fear incrementally to change your thinking. See Exercise 12: Dancing with fears in chapter 5 to walk through fear.

Situational anxiety

In this type of anxiety, triggers can be easily identifiable as they are related to specific situations. For example, it's quite common to feel situational anxiety, e.g. on your first date, before giving a speech or going up to sing in front of other people.

It's best to tackle this type of anxiety by building your self-confidence, which you can do by practising what you have to do or say beforehand. It will reduce self-doubt and uncertainty regarding the situation and, as a result, ease your nerves before the big day.

There are many more types of anxiety I could go through with you, such as; Separation Anxiety, Obsessive Compulsive Disorder, Post Traumatic Stress Disorder, Health Anxiety, and Social Anxiety. The list goes on. However, let's stay focused on why you are here. Social anxiety being what this book is about, will be elaborated on in chapter 3.

Why are some people anxious, but others aren't?

Interacting with all those people, places, and social situations looks normal and easy for everyone else. So why does it all seem to terrify you to the core?

When thinking of someone with social anxiety, people often picture a stiff, timid person glued to the corner of the room at gatherings, with their eyes down and hands and knees together. However, the opposite is also true for a lot of people. Some people with social anxiety find themselves overcompensating and being chatty and filling silences with small talk if they have to, so there's no space left for any doubts about themselves.

Not everyone's anxiety looks the same. Some might be better at hiding it, but that doesn't mean it's not there. That's just our perception. You are the most aware of the anxiety you experience and what worries you. Still, you have a far less accurate understanding of whether or not others are anxious simply because it isn't a matter discussed openly. It's still taboo to publicly discuss our doubts and fears, but why?

Aren't we all in the same boat that is this exciting, constantly changing world? Remember that when you next get in the company of others.

Some people have higher emotional sensitivity than others do, and that can make them more prone to feelings of anxiety. On another note, trauma and life-changing experiences can alter a person's brain chemistry to the point that even certain sights, sounds, smells, or tastes become associated with those bad experiences, which ingrains some of the fears they have deep within them. Highly sensitive people are also more susceptible to being impacted by emotional stress caused by difficult situations.

The primary difference why some get anxious while others don't is the thoughts and pictures they have in their mind on a minute-by-minute, hour-by-hour and day-by-day basis. As we have learned before, these thoughts create emotions, and these create how we act and behave. But unfortunately, we find it difficult to change this behaviour because the behaviour is wired deep in our subconscious mind. But what if we change the subconscious program? That would be changing the root cause and, therefore, the behaviour.

Protect me, punish me or give me attention

On a deeper level, our subconscious mind holds on to limiting behaviours such as anxiety to get the fuel it believes we need to survive. According to Rapid Transformational

Therapy (RTT) founder Marissa Peer we hold on to our limitations because our minds believe they serve some role, function, purpose or intention. (R.F.P.I. an RTT technique) (Peer 2022).

The role, function, purpose or intention is usually one of the following.

1. Protect us: stops you from doing things that may or may not benefit you for fear of embarrassing or hurting yourself.
2. Punish us: you feel you deserve it because it puts right some wrong you think you've done, so being hindered by this awful fear which harms you is karma or something like that.
3. Prioritise us: you get attention when you have an anxiety attack which makes you feel special, loved etc.

Therefore, it's crucial to ask yourself what role, function, purpose or intention the anxiety you feel is serving. If you are unsure of the answer, get present with yourself and ask how you feel when you're in a social setting and anxiety is setting in. Does the anxiety help you feel loved (safe and protected)? Does it give you significance (prioritise you)? Does it help you feel rewarded or satisfied (safe, prioritised, or sufficiently punished)? These feelings give you an idea of the purpose the anxiety you feel serves, and you will see then that the anxiety is not fit for the job you want it to do; it's only limiting you. For example, you may be reluctant to go out and meet friends because you feel you are not good enough or you don't feel loved; hence you don't feel safe. In fact, you decided again to stay home and avoid the potential hurt. Do you see, not going out to make friends keeps you from the very thing you desire? To feel love and acceptance, you must be open to meeting people who love and accept you. Even if the role of the anxiety was to punish you for some past incident you blame yourself for, the incident is in the past, so it no longer exists. Therefore, it's your thoughts of this past event that are recreating the feeling of anxiety. Then letting go of the thought is the real solution, not holding on to anxiety. So the behaviour is not fitting to helping you achieve what you need to be your best self. It may keep you sheltered, but in the long run, you are not safe; you are being controlled by a program holding you back from your awesome life.

> *Often our worst habits or behaviours are trying to fulfil an emotional purpose that they are not fit for.*
>
> — Marisa Peer

Exercise 6: Visualise to actualise

- Close your eyes and imagine yourself in a social setting that gets your heart racing, and everything in your being tells you don't go there because it stresses you out and triggers the stress response in you intensely.
- Pause within this setting and observe.
- Observe what's happening around you.
- Now observe what's happening inside of you. Do you feel safe?
- Ask yourself, what are my feelings, and why do I feel anxious?
- There is a part within you that came up with the anxiety. Ask this part of you what the purpose of the anxiety is and allow it to speak to you. Is the part there to protect you, punish you or prioritise you?
- Ask, are these feelings justified? How are they justified?
- Is the anxiety helping you or inhibiting you?
- What is it costing you to allow this feeling to remain?
- What is the thought that's causing this anxiety?
- Can you prove the thought is true?
- How else could you try to see things and think to change your feelings?

- **Can you ask the part of you that created the anxiety to let it go?**
- **If it doesn't want to let go of the anxiety, ask it to take up a new supporting role. Instead of making you feel anxious and shutting you down. Maybe it could be your cheerleader, mentor, or best friend giving you more positive thoughts. It must take on an empowering role to get you excited about being free to be yourself.**
- **Ask yourself; Are you ready to let the anxiety go? Let it go.**
- **Practice this daily in your mind and when ready, put yourself in a physical setting that would generally get you anxious and as you did in your mind, be mindful of the same questions. Observe any anxious feelings as above without any judgment. Stay present and aware.**

This technique is massively effective under hypnosis, i.e. in a deeply relaxed state. Parts of this technique are used by therapists, including Rapid Transformational Therapists like myself. If the part of you that created the anxiety does not want to let go, it may be a good idea to see an RTT therapist to help you successfully through this process.

Chapter 3
What is social anxiety?
Why do I feel this way?

> *But if I am in an unfamiliar place, among a number of strange people, or people whom I feel to be strangers, then the whole room presses on my chest and I am unable to move, my whole personality seems virtually to get under their skins, and everything becomes hopeless.*
>
> — Franz Kafka

On the surface, it may not seem like social interaction is all that threatening. It's not like all those people are going to bite, right? That's the thing about phobias, though; most of the time, what you are scared of does not even put you in any danger, but that doesn't make you any less anxious. You probably know better than anyone else that this fear is totally irrational and unnecessary. But let's see what social anxiety is about and where it comes from

A psychological disorder is a dysfunctional pattern of thoughts, feelings, or behaviours that severely impact one's ability to live a healthy life.

Chances are that many people you have spoken to may be struggling with social anxiety to some degree. Some people, though they have low self-esteem can hide it exceptionally well and wear a suit of confidence that disguises what they actually feel on the inside and feel about themselves. Others have lived with it long enough to become familiar with it and have developed coping skills. The point is social anxiety is a very common issue, usually "self-diagnosed". Being nervous before an audition, an interview, an exam or meeting new people does not mean you have social anxiety though; that's just being human. However, social situations that cause the person extreme distress and lead them to cope with their pain in ways that they may not even realise are unhealthy, qualify as a disorder.

Social anxiety disorder is from the same world as that of phobias. As a socially anxious person, even the thought of being at a gathering can kickstart bouts of worrying, insecurities and unwavering irrational fear of specific activities, situations or objects. These unhealthy thinking patterns eventually lead to avoidance behaviours such as withdrawing. On top of that, you may or may not be aware that the same avoidance behaviours you use to feel safe and comfortable reinforce your anxiety.

Signs and symptoms

Why am I so awkward? Am I just shy, or could it be more? Do I have social anxiety?

The following are some signs and symptoms of social anxiety disorder:

- Avoiding group activities.
- Fear of embarrassment caused by anxious symptoms showing, such as sweating, stammering or shaky voice.
- Fear that others can see 'through you' or notice that you look anxious.
- Frequent protests against meeting new people or going to social gatherings.
- Physical symptoms of anxiety during social interaction, such as rapid heart rate and breathing, tight feeling in the chest, feeling flushed, etc.

In general, socially anxious people fear trying because they're scared they'll be judged and make a fool out of themselves.

See if any of the following sound familiar:

- Feeling self-conscious while walking into class or down the street. You start to think you're walking 'funny', that your arms look weird when they are by your side, so you put your hands in your pockets, wait no, that felt weird too. "Should I cross them?" "No, I hate how that feels". "Who the hell crosses their arms while they're walking?"
- When other people laugh, you feel like they're laughing at you. "What did I do?" "Are they laughing at me?" "Is there something on my face?" "I have to get out of here quickly."
- People think you're rude, cold, or intimidating. It's hard for you to stop and make small talk. Little do they know that all you can afford to do is smile and nod because you believe your voice will shake if you speak or you're scared you'll say something embarrassing.
- You have to throw away your used tissue, or you need to excuse yourself to the toilet. You're scared that when you get up, everyone's going to watch you. You choose to stay put.
- You avoid picking up calls or you turn your screen off when your phone starts to ring. Something about calls makes your stomach churn.
- You can't place an order at restaurants.

- You don't feel like going to school when the only friend you have isn't going.
- Going for a walk alone.
- The teacher asks a question, and you know the answer, but you would never put your hand up, fearing any attention you may attract.

Causes and triggers

> *Your mind listens to your innermost thoughts and responds to what you are thinking, it has no choice but to do what you tell it to.*
>
> — Thashna Walsh

Genetics and brain chemistry

A biological reason is often found behind psychological issues. For example, some scientific research explains that one of the causes of anxiety might be inherited genes, meaning that it might be possible that anxiety disorders run in the family and you got it from your parents. Genes determine your entire make-up, and each has various possibilities of what feature it gives you. Seventeen genes have been identified with anxiety-related expressions (Donner & Pirkola, 2008).

I agree; some people seem naturally more anxious than others and according to research, are likely to pass that on to their kids. Those with one or both parents being anxious may also have the anxiety trait. For instance, a parent that has avoided meeting relatives and having guests over or never liked going out to meet friends can have a child with the same anxious tendencies. However, is this genetic, or is it environmental?

Other research on identical twins showed that when one twin has a particular phobia, the other twin has a 30% chance of developing the same phobia (Villafuerte 2003). That said, blaming genetics for social anxiety issues can feel as if there is nothing that can be done about it, and you will have to be this way forever. Thankfully, more recent studies by Dr Bruce Lipton have proven through the science of epigenetics that changing your lifestyle, environment, thoughts, and behaviours can down-regulate the genes and rewrite the genome responsible for many illnesses (Lipton 2006). In other words, you are not doomed by your genes to suffer from social anxiety forever. You can change and be better.

Environmental factors: Upbringing and early life

Factors such as parents being unfit for their roles, that are abusive toward their children also contribute to the development of social anxiety within the child. A child who has grown up hearing taunts and being discouraged by their caregivers or family members will be far more predisposed to having low self-esteem and greater anxiety levels. Children who are victims of physical or emotional abuse naturally lose trust in most people as they don't receive the love and care they need from those responsible for caring for them. Instead, those who are meant to protect them have abused their position. Fights at home, divorced parents or domestic violence, physical and psychological trauma will impact any child or adolescent seeing or experiencing it. For these children, this creates the idea that the world is inherently a scary, uncertain and unsafe place where people aren't to be trusted. They may also conclude that it's their fault and therefore they must be unloveable or something is wrong with them.

Triggers

Certain situations, actions, or events that are reminders of a traumatic or unpleasant past that lead to intense feelings of fear and distress are known as triggers.

You might do your best to avoid things that may trigger you whenever you can help it, such as:

- avoiding conversations with authority figures,
- skipping parties and large family gatherings,
- not sharing your phone number because calls make you anxious
- not going to places where you are almost sure you won't know anyone.

You avoid these because you think of the outcome and the extreme discomfort you could feel, which could build up to an anxiety attack.

As mentioned before, an anxiety attack is the onset of intense feelings of fear that develop very quickly. It is accommodated by physical symptoms such as increased heart rate, nausea, sweating, shaking and hyperventilation and is caused by triggers. Your thoughts can get mixed up, you can't figure out what's happening around you, and you struggle with catching your breath.

The key to grounding yourself is recognising that your thoughts have started this. So, focusing on your breathing will help empty your mind of the thoughts driving the feeling. When you can control the pace of your breathing, you are also making sure your brain gets enough oxygen to calm it down. So, breathing exercises give you a greater capacity for making better decisions.

Here are 5 steps to find relief when triggered and you can feel anxiety approaching. This technique is not an ultimate cure, but this will help ground you into reality and calm you down by warding off unwanted thoughts, emotions and feelings resulting from triggers. Let's start.

Exercise 7: Off The Trigger Calming Technique - 5...4... 3...2...1...

- Take slow, deep breaths. Using the 4-7-8 breathing count, close your lips and breathe in through your nose, counting to 4. Hold your breath for a count of 7, then breathe out for a count of 8 seconds. Continue this rhythm of breathing.
- Point out 5 things you can SEE. Poster on the wall, a chair, a pen holder, the sky or a stack of books. Spot any 5 things and acknowledge them.
- Pick up 4 items so you can TOUCH and feel each one for its texture. Your water bottle, your laptop, phone, wallet or your own hands.
- Listen for 3 things around you that you can HEAR. Maybe it can be the pitter-patter of the rain against the window, birds chirping, cars passing, or music playing in the background.
- Find 2 things that you can SMELL. This can be difficult if you are someplace where you don't exactly have a lot of stimuli or don't have a lot of smells. Perhaps you can go to the nearest bathroom and smell some soap, check how your shirt smells, find a fragrance if you are at home or cut a fresh lemon.
- End the exercise by finding 1 thing you can TASTE. Chewing gum, sipping water and swishing

it in your mouth or getting yourself something light to eat.

- **Take a deep breath and notice that you have calmed yourself by distracting yourself into the present moment. Do you see how easy it easy to change your path of thinking?**

You have diffused yourself simply with this calming 5-4-3-2-1 technique. You can pat yourself on the back and smile.

More importantly, by doing this exercise, you will have distracted yourself from your thoughts and released yourself from them. Engaging all five senses is the ultimate distraction and gives you a chance to start over with better thoughts and feelings while introducing new behaviours to your subconscious mind.

Other contributory factors

The challenges of being a teenager:

Everyone has their fair share of challenges; who's to say you don't get to have your own? Your parents might tell you that you have it way easier than they did when they were your age. However, they forget that you are your own person, with insecurities of your own and challenges that no one else would truly know about unless they are exceptional empaths.

Parents and guardians:

As much as you love your parents and see that they only want to be there for you through your difficult times, you may probably agree that you've often felt more misunderstood by them and feel that they just "don't get it". You probably think it'd be nice if they quit forcing you to be top of your class all the time or nagging you about tidying your room and actually listened to you for a change. Hey, it's alright. Just because you feel like other people, including your parents, wouldn't understand your problems, it doesn't mean you give up on others or yourself. The two most common mental health problems in adolescents are anxiety and depression (Granic 2020). So, your struggles are valid, and you should know that first and foremost. However, know this, there are people who are willing to listen and genuinely help you. If you have parents who will listen and help you without judgement, you are one of the lucky ones, so go to them and allow them to help. If you feel you don't have this luxury, going to your school counsellor may provide guidance if you have one. Don't knock it till you have tried it. They have to keep your conversations confidential so talk to them. You can also contact organisations such as 'The Samaritans', an online mental health help resource, via email, phone or letter. Mental health awareness is much more prevalent nowadays, and there are many more places to get help. It's very important to get help and not suffer in silence. Alternatively, if you are not in immediate danger to yourself or others, keep reading to reveal more power tools for your toolkit.

School:

School is challenging with the constant pressure of exams, expectations from adults to do well academically, feeling self-conscious and struggling to fit in or join a group of your own friends. It feels like everyone else is doing great, but you just can't seem to do enough. Under so much academic pressure, many students become convinced that their grades ultimately determine their worth. Consequently, leading to extreme burnout and prolonged feelings of stress that can build up to anxiety.

It starts feeling like there is never enough time to get everything done. You have to juggle so many responsibilities that all require your time and energy. In addition, you have to show up like you have it all under control when you are really screaming inside.

Breathe; it's ok. Everyone is going through it, and you will get through it stronger if you choose to see the growth to be had.

Hormones and Body Image:

Appearance and body image all play an essential part in your identity. It has to do with how you view yourself physically, your size, shape, your facial features and how you feel others view you physically. You compare yourself with others and, in many cases put them on a pedestal and put yourself down if you suffer from low self-esteem. For many teens, self-image is the leading cause of their insecurities because poor self-image may result in negative emotions of not feeling that they are good enough, pretty enough, cool enough, rich enough and so on. How about recognising your unique qualities and falling in love with yourself just the way you are? You could learn to do this. It's vital to understand this, as being dissatisfied with your self-image can lead to other troubles, such as eating disorders and depression. A person with low self-esteem is susceptible to the comments and opinions of others. They may succumb to peer pressure, feeling pressured to dress a certain way, join certain clubs, hang out at certain spots, drink alcohol, smoke cigarettes and take drugs, even when they don't want to. Others pretend to be someone they are not while forcing themselves to fit in so they won't be excluded or picked on as different. They also depend on the protection from the group of peers they are hanging out with. Another set of people may become withdrawn so as not to get noticed at all, reducing their chances of being bullied.

At home, some parents might not even be aware that their comments on what their teenage sons and daughters are eating or wearing can also impact their self-esteem. They think they are being helpful by pointing out these things, but these judgmental comments can hurt.

Again remember, all teenagers are going through changes. The important thing is to embrace the changes as you are developing into an adult, and the process is a beautiful gift. Life becomes easier when you let go of resistance and welcome natural changes. I am not trying to diminish your feelings; however, if you realise all teenagers, including and especially those that call themselves the 'popular ones', are experiencing the very same thing as you. The only way to feel empowered is to accept yourself as you are because we are all the same, even if we appear different. Set yourself free from the worry of what your body is doing and what others may be thinking and focus on your thoughts about yourself and treat yourself with love and respect. You have the power to think what you want, which gives you all the power you need to be free.

Social media and anxiety dilemma:

If you aren't able to gauge your social media consumption, it can be like the fuel to the social anxiety you are experiencing, which is an already raging flame. Social media is a platform where every other user is sure to showcase only the golden, pristine aspects of their lives. Retouched selfies and photos, putting up videos of themselves at parties and lively gatherings as proof that they have a rich life. People are selective about what they share online. It's like their own public portfolio that shows how 'cool' they are, and successful people are most likely to share the happy parts or what gives the illusion of happiness. Can you see where this is going? Teens are bound to subconsciously compare their lives with those of others that they see on the screen. At a time when they are supposed to be growing through challenges and learning to tackle new opportunities, gain new experiences, and familiarise themselves with change. In a time when they are meant to figure out who they are and be true to themselves, they are being influenced more by the lives of others online who don't even know themselves.

"Why can't I be popular like that guy from my class? He gets all the girls in school."

Social media warps your perception of what a good, fulfilling life is. It makes you think you must look and act a certain way, follow the latest trends, go to certain places, and have many friends to be relevant. But, unfortunately, people are rarely self-aware and are far too wrapped up in their social network to stop and think, "Is this affecting my mental well-being? Is this making me think differently about myself?"

Honestly, I get it. The internet has been a blessing in some cases because it has become a platform for anxious people who do not find it easy to talk about their anxiety face to face. They can now find an online community or outlet where they can discuss, research and express their issues through various media. Social media also serves the purposes of staying in touch with friends, discovering new niches, connecting with people, maintaining old relationships, etc. All this is good, but if it is unmanaged, it can foster a very negative side.

Cyberbullying, stress, negative self-image, poor time management skills and addiction are some negative aspects of social media. There is also an increasing concern about how addictive social media has become. Look around you at lunch. What is everyone doing? Yes, most people are glued to their phones and not talking to each other.

The socially anxious may find the online space comfortable, so they adjust well behind the screen, finding their place of solace - safe and hidden. As a result, they may become dependent on social media and online messaging platforms. However, the online world is not reality. Relying on social media and online friends rather than making real-world connections further alienates you. Instead, you watch the world go by without you, as you feel even worse with time, believing that you can't fit in or are not good enough. That, of course, is not the truth about you.

So, as you navigate the roots and nature of social anxiety, remember to consider the potential harms of the digital world of social media. There is a documentary film on Netflix that you should take some time to watch called 'The Social Dilemma'. It shows how social media is designed to nurture an addiction to it while maximising profit. It shows how teens are being manipulated and the detrimental effects of social media on their mental health. Most of the top techs and employees have admitted that they do not allow their own children to use certain social networking platforms due to the harm they know they can cause.

At the end of the day

There is one common factor residing in all these contributors to social anxiety. Do you know what it is? It's the one thing you control. Your thoughts. We are going to embark on a journey on how to think better, feel better and have a better experience of life. Your freedom lies pages away, but you gotta take your spirit of action with it. Skip the page and let's get to it.

Chapter 4
The battle for your mind
Realistic thinking trumps fear

> *You can have excuses or results, not both*
>
> — Unknown

You think you are not good enough, which causes social anxiety, which makes you doubt yourself and your abilities and perpetuates the anxiety. This keeps you stuck in a loop of visualising and thinking negative thoughts about the worst that could happen.

Here are examples of negative thoughts perhaps you may be able to relate to:

- "I'll say the wrong thing, and others will get offended."
- "Everyone will have someone to talk to except me."

- "I'm not nearly as good-looking or smart as others. Who would possibly like me?"
- "Others are going to judge me and how stupid I look."
- "What if I get so nervous that I cannot move or speak? What will others think?"
- "I'm too boring. No one wants to talk to me."
- "What if I forget everything I have to say?"
- "Other people will notice that I look nervous and point it out."

Here are a few questions for you. Where do you see the fact in all of these thoughts? What proof do you have that any of this is true? There is no proof that these negative thoughts are true. Developing realistic thinking is one of the top ways to overcome social anxiety. This exercise focuses on realistic thinking. Get your journal out; let's work through this.

Step 1: Identify and list down your negative thoughts and fears

It's difficult in the moment to deduce how you judge yourself when in triggering situations, e.g. when you are talking to someone new or giving a presentation in class, you may feel terrified or embarrassed and not in the frame of mind to analyse your feelings in the moment. So, practise observing and noting down your fears before being in the actual situation. This will help you grow healthier mechanisms for coping.

When you are ready and up for a challenge, believe in your strength and start interacting with more people. I don't mean meeting crowds every day, but you can talk to someone in your class who you find interesting or think is nice. It might be uncomfortable, and you won't feel like doing it, but that is the point. So note down your thoughts before proceeding, and go up to the person and face your fear! Deep breath, believe in yourself and do it. However it goes, note down your concerns and thoughts afterward.

Step 2: Evaluate the negative thoughts you noted down

Evaluating the negative thoughts is a learning experience and a way to get to know yourself better and how you think. Read over your notes and look at them with a fresh perspective: they are not based on any FACTS. They are 'what-ifs', 'maybe's' and 'unlikely possibilities'. They are not set in stone. How can you be so sure you'll mess up if you don't even try?

Once you understand that, think of helpful thoughts in the future that can motivate you before finding yourself in similar situations.

Here is an exercise to help you the next time you find yourself imagining a scenario where you are having troublesome thoughts that are getting in your way. First, ask yourself questions to identify and understand them and turn them around.

Exercise 8: Taking down the adversary

Write down the statement of what you think will go wrong and what people will think about you. Then under it, write the answers to the following questions.

- **How sure am I that this will happen?**
- **Has this happened before? How many times?**
- **What proof do I have that this will happen?**
- **Does this person's/these people's opinions decide my future?**
- **If one person thinks this about me, does that mean everyone else will think the same?**
- **Is what people think my responsibility?**
- **What can I do to cope or handle the situation if something bad happens?**
- **How can I prepare for such a situation in the future?**
- **What would I say to a friend if they had such thoughts?**

Write a more positive statement of what could also potentially happen.

You will want to make excuses while doing this exercise. However, pretend the excuses did not exist. What will you think and do then? Also, don't allow yourself to tell you "I don't know". When you think you don't know, ask yourself "If I did know, then what would the answer be?" Your subconscious mind will hold you captive if you let it, so, it is up to you to buckle down, feel it out and come up with the answers. When you do this, you are teaching yourself who you truly are and also teaching your subconscious mind what makes sense to hold on to and what does not.

Rules of the battlefield

Your mind is the battlefield on which you manoeuvre through your life every day. By focusing on negative thoughts, anxiety takes control. Yes, you have given anxious thoughts control over you. Your thoughts create the pictures in your mind of the worst-case scenario. This focus screams danger to your subconscious mind. Your mind then plays out the recording or memory of how you should feel and behave based on some old redundant behaviours that once served you. How we overcome this mind control is to understand the simple rules your mind plays by - always and without fail.

You can learn to focus your thoughts, or you can let an old program in your mind control you. Learn to distinguish between helpful and positive thoughts and thoughts that just aren't doing you any good. Though your mind is naturally wired to lean towards what is familiar and comfortable because it believes it's in your best interest, do not forget that our mind is yours to influence. You can get it to work for you as long as you understand it and use it properly. Your mind picks up on all the thoughts you focus on. It listens closely to you and believes what you think and say about yourself, whether it's good or bad or true or not. It just pays attention to what you pay attention to, period.

So if you continue to think that you aren't good enough and won't do well in life, you'll remain stuck on this hamster wheel of self-deprecation as a slave to your negative, destructive thoughts. Can you tell where you need to set up your mental construction site right now? Where do you need to start working? Yes, it's your thoughts. I have been saying it since the start of the book.

You want to befriend yourself. Sit down, breathe deep and speak to yourself with love and kindness from now on. Then, start untangling the bundle of cables and follow them to your mind's dashboard. You remember that you can't just pull the anxiety plugs and expect to have the positive transformation you're looking for because of your subconscious programming. So, let's look at the programs and rules your mind seems to be following.

Like you can exercise your physical body to build muscle, you can exercise your mind muscles to strengthen them. Initially, as with any physical exertion, it will be exhausting, and you will feel resistance. However, you build strength as you continue to push yourself a little extra with each focused attempt. Your mind will accept the challenge and adapt.

However, sometimes all you need to do is to sit and listen to yourself. Understand the balance between challenging yourself, listening to yourself and respecting your limits. Let the thoughts pass instead of straining yourself, observe their energy and where you are holding that energy in your body. According to Marisa Peer, when dealing with the subconscious mind, the greater the conscious effort, the less the subconscious responds [21]. Meaning you cannot fight the programs by yelling at them. That would be like yelling at your Alexa, saying, "Hey google!" and expecting Alexa to respond. She won't, as she is programmed to respond to her name, Alexa and not Google. According to Dr Joe Dispenza, using the same frequency of conscious effort that created the issue to override a subconscious problem causes more harm to your brain than good. It's like throwing fuel on a flame. So the only way to change is to get to the subconscious level by slowing the brain waves down, finding the root cause of the faulty thinking, weeding it out and planting a new and more productive thought conducive to the happiness you deserve.

Mind rules

- Once the subconscious mind has accepted an idea, it remains until another idea replaces it.
- The strongest force in humans is that we must act in a way that consistently matches our thinking.
- Every thought you think causes a physical reaction and an emotional response within you.

- Imagination is more powerful than knowledge. Therefore, in a battle between emotion and logic, emotion always wins.
- Your mind does what you focus on.
- Your mind works to move you from pain to pleasure even when the pleasure is not practical long term, like avoidance behaviour.
- Your mind is wired to resist what is unfamiliar and to return to what is familiar. This is why changing is difficult.
- Your mind does not care if what you tell it is good, bad, true, false, healthy, unhealthy or right or wrong. It accepts and acts on your thoughts, words and emotions regardless.
- You make your beliefs; then your beliefs create your choices/actions/energy, making those beliefs real.
- What you present to your mind, your mind will present back to you.
- When dealing with the subconscious mind, the greater the conscious effort, the less the subconscious responds.
- The mind cannot hold conflicting beliefs or thoughts that cancel each other out. Like wanting to change and go out and meet friends, but fearful thoughts hold you back to keep you safe from hurt, so you stay home.
- Your mind can only work in the present tense. Therefore when you think about something terrible

potentially happening, your mind thinks it is happening there and then.

- Your mind does not recognise words like don't, can't, no, not, later, maybe, tomorrow or yesterday. It exists only in the present moment, in the now. It just IS.
- Your mind can only respond to words that make pictures, the more vivid the picture, the more powerful the response.
- Your mind responds better (healthier) to positive words and to specific detailed dynamic (picture forming) words and instructions.
- The mind learns by repetition. Studies show it takes 21 days to form a new neural network in the brain to support a new idea. After 90 days of practice, the idea becomes hardwired and automated.
- What is expected tends to be realised. Whatever you focus on, you get more of it.

Some people can get super aware and stay on top of where they are focusing their thoughts and find their way to the other side of social and other anxieties. However, this takes a considerable amount of time, mental effort, self-awareness and healing along the way. Slowing your mind down to access the subconscious mind is a skill I recommend you develop. Hypnotherapists help you to slow your mind down so they can help you enter your subconscious mind to find the root cause of your negative thoughts and actions. I use the techniques of Rapid Transformational Therapy (Chapter 8), which uses hypnosis to help my clients. It is extremely fast and effective. The breathing techniques in this book (Chapter 6) also slow your mind down to give you some relief. A relaxed mind can't be anxious at the same time. A relaxed mind works efficiently and in the present moment. A relaxed mind is rational and makes positive and healthy choices.

Win the battle

Meditation is a mental practice for relaxing the body and the mind. It slows down the brain waves to put you in a state of ease. It doesn't take much effort. You need only to be present, which is being free from distractions and engaging only with what is happening with you in the moment. A socially anxious mind turns you against yourself because you are trying to control too many thoughts at once, leaving you out of control and doubting your abilities. Because negative thinking is based on worst-case outcomes, you are clearly not living in the present but in the future based on the past.

What I mean by this is, you imagine the worst that could happen based on memories of your past or someone else's. Can you remember a time when something happened to you or someone else, and you or that person got laughed at and felt embarrassed? Do you remember the feeling you had, or you had on their behalf? So now, when you consider going out with friends to a party, you may think of all the scenarios where it could all go wrong based on that past event. You could get embarrassed and laughed at, so you avoid going to protect yourself from those horrible feelings of vulnerability. You are not living in the present moment but in the future based on past memories. You could go to the party and have a wonderful time; however, you don't think of that potential, hence the perpetuated anxiety. This negative state drains your energy and clouds your thinking. Maybe you can't barricade the negative thoughts; it's okay. In fact, you can't control the 70,000 thoughts we have on average each day. However, you can choose the ones you give your attention to. The purpose of meditating is to change how you relate to your thoughts, change them for better thoughts and allow new feelings to come up that are more supportive of the outcome you truly want. It will gain you the knack of being able to focus, be more self-aware, and shift your focus to positive thoughts instead of negative ones.

Meditation helps bring awareness to your mind without force, letting you ease into the present moment and ask, "How do I feel right now?" Not fighting or resisting negative thoughts and emotions but simply letting them pass as clouds in the sky. To resist anything, you have to interact and focus on it. Therefore, resisting negative thoughts traps you into thinking even more about them, and as what you focus on, you get more of, the very thing you resist, finds you. Energy flows where attention goes. So, chose better ones and let the negative thoughts go.

Meditation enables us to shift from higher-frequency brain waves to lower frequency, which activates and amplifies specific areas of your brain and turns down the volume of other areas. Consequently, allowing you to tap into your subconscious mind, correct limiting beliefs and accept better suggestions, which opens you up to a life free from any form of anxiety. All in all, your emotional health will improve, followed by your social life and your physical well-being.

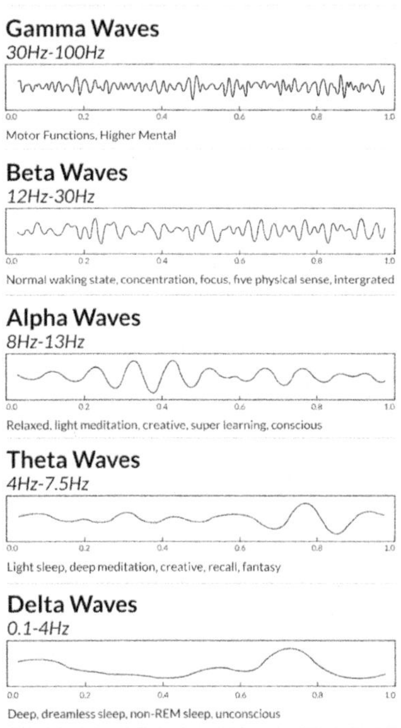

Diagram 5: *Demonstrates brain wave frequencies and functions.*

Take a look at the diagram above.

Delta is sleep mode in adults and children, where the body is restoring itself, and there is very little conscious awareness. Notice how slow the brain waves are?

At age 2 to 5 or 6, a child's brain is in Theta brain wave mode, the state of accepting, being open, observant, and taking everything in subconsciously as they start connecting with their outside world and storing the information without much thought. This is a child's world of extraordinary imagination. There is little to no analytical thinking in this state, so children at this age accept what you tell them.

Theta is the state in which we are most programmable. Hypnotherapists often access the subconscious mind in this state. In this state, the conscious mind is awake while the subconscious mind sleeps. In meditating, this state is where you want to get to in order to make the changes you need to create the life you want.

From ages 5 to 8, the analytical mind starts to form, and children begin to make conclusions about their outer and inner worlds. Both their outer world and inner world of imagination are real to them, so they are great at pretending. They are in the Alpha state at this stage.

Alpha in adults is the state of shutting out the sensory data by closing your eyes and going within. It's a state of relaxation, focusing on your thoughts and making them more real than what is happening outside of you; a state of daydreaming. We enter this state intermittently throughout the day when we take information in to think about and consider.

Can you see how easy it is to condition someone's mind to a belief? Especially children between the ages of 0 to 8. Without that ability to analyse what they are being taught or to block the information from their subconscious mind, they don't stand a chance if constantly exposed to negative experiences. So, if your low self-confidence and self-esteem have been with you for as long as you can remember, you were more than likely conditioned at a young age.

Exercise 9: Let's Meditate

- **Find a quiet place where there are no distractions. Set a timer for 10 minutes.**
- **Sit on a chair with your feet flat on the ground and your spine straight and upright. Or, sit on the floor with your legs crossed in the lotus position. Or, Lay down flat on your back, legs straight and naturally apart, hands straight down the sides of you with your palms facing upward. Make sure your shoulders are open and relaxed.**
- **Become aware of your breathing and establish a gentle, deep, slow pattern.**
- **Breathe in through your nose and out through your mouth.**

- Breathe in again and feel the air entering your nostril, lungs, and chest.
- Feel your belly fill up with air and as your chest expands and as you breathe out, notice how your muscles all over your body start to let go and relax now.
- Close your eyes to turn your awareness within.
- Continue breathing
- Notice how your body feels, starting from the top. Notice any tension in your brow, jaw, and face and release it. Breathing deeply in and on the out-breath, letting go of any tension in your head.
- Repeat this as you move your attention to your neck and shoulders, breathing and letting go of any tightness.
- Move your attention to your chest and torso, breathing and letting tension fall away.
- Move now to your abdomen and back. Easily and gently allowing yourself to drift into deep relaxation.
- Let the muscles of your pelvis and thighs relax and let go of all tension. Breathe deeply and fully, then breathe out all stress and tightness.
- Focus on your breathing. When you start to notice your mind wandering, that's ok. Let your thoughts pass freely and gently bring your attention back to your breathing. Be kind to yourself.

- **Continue; bring your awareness to your legs and feet; sense any tension floating away. As you breathe deeply and completely.**
- **Finally, bring your awareness to your entire body. Feel the energy inside your body. Feel the looseness, the ease, the relaxation.**
- **Take a few long breaths in and out to saturate your entire body with fresh air now, and as you breathe out, allow your entire body from the top of your head to the tips of your toes to sink and let go into deep surrender.**
- **Close your meditation with softness and compassion for yourself. You are ok, and your mind wants to support you; it is with you.**
- **Trust that your mind already knows the answers you need, and when you take it to this deep state of peace, it will always support you back to your true self.**
- **You have started your journey back to you. Open your eyes.**

Sometimes during meditation, you may feel sleepy, this is natural. It means you are slowing your brain waves down successfully. It's the point between being wide awake and sleeping that you are working to get to so, stay present with the sleepy feeling as you do the meditation. If it is safe to do so, you may fall asleep after you are finished.

Find your free guided hypnotic meditation link below:

Relax and rewire meditation intro:

https://drive.google.com/file/d/1ScYleMMz-4uzDrltXesv-CwnLUVJntsy6/view?usp=sharing

Relax and rewire meditation:

https://drive.google.com/file/d/1MlNLqzmz5TNOQpD-Cv6ERTIJVosjUUEh_/view?usp=sharing

Chapter 5
Strategise to overcome
The Coping Skills Toolkit

> *"From now on, start asking yourself WHY you feel a certain way, WHAT made you perform a certain action, and HOW you could do things differently. The information you discover is powerful because it helps you to discover patterns and in turn use your mind productively and efficiently. After all, your mind is your most powerful tool, but it's not useful if you don't know how to use it. It's like trying to fix a printer with a stapler: it doesn't work. Trust me, I've tried."*
>
> — Lilly Singh

Social anxiety is tricky. It feels like a cage, and you're trapped in it by some invisible force.

Being mentally and emotionally prepared with a toolkit of coping skills will help you feel more secure. Instead of dreading social situations, be reassured that you have what you need to stay calm and collected. This chapter includes multiple exercises and sections to encourage positive changes and behaviours by utilising healthy coping mechanisms and skills.

Let's help you assemble your very own toolkit. So, sit back with your notebook/journal and pen and master the coming exercises.

Affirm it

Your thoughts cause your emotional state; your emotions determine your actions; this goes full circle and comes back to your thoughts being either affirmed or denied. You learned that in chapter 1, remember? So, when you are feeling rubbish and defeated, that feeling is fostered by rubbish and defeating thoughts, resulting in you making half-hearted efforts and taking half-hearted actions or none at all. That gets you nowhere, and you stay stuck in a rut.

What if you could harness the negative energy you feel and convert it to become something that can benefit you? Develop healthy and positive self-talk through positive affirmations.

The mind learns by repeated information. For example, to get good at sports, cooking, playing an instrument, acrobatics, video games and so on, you have to practice. The more you do it, the easier it becomes, and over time it becomes second nature.

Positive affirmations are positive sets of phrases and statements you repeat to yourself to help you overpower, even erase the negative thoughts that haunt you to encourage helpful, positive thinking. Create a healthier inner guide and let your natural, happier self come out and shine. By thinking and seeing yourself in a positive light, you start to attract positive energy that empowers you to face people, grasp opportunities and revel in your achievements.

It's not an overnight fix but a habit worth building because every confident, self-assured human being uses positive affirmations consciously or unconsciously. They are exercises for your brain. They rewire the negative subconscious behaviours with new productive and positive ones and keep you focused. However, for affirmations to work, you must understand that, just saying the words won't work. To make an impression on your subconscious mind, you must generate the feelings behind what you say. It's the only way to get the truth of the affirmation inside your body (the subconscious mind). Put another way, the subconscious mind is the feeling mind, requiring feelings to make an impression on it.

Here is an example. The affirmation: "**I am fun and interesting, and people want to get to know me**".

Now, you can look at yourself in the mirror or close your eyes as you say your affirmations. Remember, you are saying them to yourself, who listens subconsciously. You need to listen and take it in and feel yourself taking it in, believing it. There is just you and yourself, so go all in. It may feel silly to start, but the gains far outweigh your discomfort.

So, as you say your affirmation, see yourself in your mind being fun and interesting, see people around you smile with you, and you smile with them, and you feel good inside. This imagery creation is called visualisation. It is the glue that holds everything together. If you are doing it right, you should feel pretty good in the end. If you don't, keep working at it, you will break through. Do your affirmations daily, repeating the one most fitting for you at least 20 times, more if you like. You can repeat this as often as you like throughout each day, but go all in and do it properly.

After finishing your affirmation, keep the thoughts active with you throughout the day, regardless of what may be happening.

> *Repetition is the mother of all skills.*
>
> — Tony Robbins

Here are some affirmations below you could use. You can also write your own. If you write your own, ensure they are written in the present tense and use only cheerful and colourful words.

Exercise 10: Positive affirmations for social anxiety

- **I am fully capable of interacting and making positive connections with those around me.**
- **Everyone here is just like me. We all have a lot in common.**
- **I set my own pace in interacting with others. It is a calm, chilled, safe and fun space.**
- **I don't have a motive when I am meeting new people. I'm free and safe to settle in and enjoy myself.**
- **I speak up, introduce myself and ask questions. People love getting to know me; it is so much fun.**
- **I am secure in myself; I feel safe as I meet and get to know people.**
- **I am excited about making new friends/meeting new people/going to the party tonight. I will have so much fun.**
- **I feel so calm here with people; I sit back and take it all in, feeling safe, heard, and appreciated.**
- **I am confident in myself and my abilities.**
- **I am calm and secure and feel comfortable in my own skin.**

- **There is nothing I can control except my own thoughts, and I control them with beautiful, positive, empowering visualisations of fun, flow and belonging.**

Caring what YOU think

Rue checks her phone to see the time. 2:09 AM. She hasn't been able to sleep since she went to bed. The longer it takes for her to fall asleep, the more stressed she feels since she hates going to school tired. She thinks that others must be able to tell when she's tired, which embarrasses her because she knows it gives her the "resting bitch face" look. She doesn't want to come off as "rude" or a "snob."

"Guess I'll have to wear more concealer than usual. I run out of it so quickly. Most of it is spent trying to cover my pimples."

She realized that she had been torturing herself for hours on end, thinking about what everyone in her class must think of her. How she talks, walks, rarely speaks to anyone first, disappears at break time, and doesn't like working in groups. She especially hates when she can't read loud enough in class when it's her turn to read, so her teacher continuously interrupts her, "Louder, Rue. I can't hear you!" Her eyes well up with tears just thinking about that.

She feels all alone and lonely. Will she ever have a best friend? Will she ever have her first date? Would anyone even like her enough to want anything to do with her?

It's only been two months since she started at her new school, but she feels so alienated. She wonders, will she ever be accepted?

The time is now 2:45 AM. She switches sides, grabs her phone and opens TikTok in an attempt to take her mind off things. Admittedly, she's miserable and doesn't know what to do to help herself.

Okay, Rue. That's some seriously harsh judgment toward yourself, but I can understand. We are our own worst critics. We judge ourselves before anyone else can judge us. Why do we do that, though? Why can't we be more kind and more understanding of ourselves?

We need to feel accepted by others for our survival. It's a primitive instinct that was very useful in the primitive days when we depended on being accepted into clans, groups or communities to survive. When members got exiled or abandoned, they would most likely die of exhaustion, starvation or being caught as prey. So when we face rejection or embarrassment, we feel the same pain and fear of being vulnerable, deemed an outcast or a misfit.

If you often think about conversations and interactions you have had in the past and wish you had said or done something differently, it could mean that you get easily affected by what others think of you. You want to fit in and be accepted and included.

Of course, it is important to care about what others think. That is how you learn, experience, gain understanding and grow. You get to glean from others, learn your opinions, likes, dislikes and how to develop your self-image based on your own intrinsic values. However, when you care too much about what others think of you, you put yourself under pressure to perform well for them and not yourself. In your mind, you may even exaggerate what others think of you, whether it's good or bad, especially the bad, instead of feeling comfortable enough to be your remarkable and unique self.

What others think of you is their own opinion and perception; frankly, it should be none of your business, especially if they think negatively about you when they don't even know you. This small-minded thinking makes no sense, and you should care less about their opinions.

Often people overcompensate for their own insecurities and may look confident on the outside. Social anxiety can present in many ways. So be kinder to yourself because most of your peers are just as worried and feeling just as lost, trying to figure things out just like you. Be honest with yourself and be kind to yourself and everyone else. The only person's opinion of you that you should be concerned with is yours.

People who are mean or bullies who may pick on you are the most insecure. They struggle with dealing with their emotions and take it out externally on others. So it's nothing to do with you and everything to do with them not understanding how to go within themselves to find the answers like you are doing now. So maybe you could buy them this book anonymously as they more than likely need it too.

At a certain age, your parents or guardians of course have a strong influence over you and have a say in what you do but not with regard to how you feel. Your feelings are yours, your opinions are yours and you should feel free to have them and voice them when you want and with respect.

Where you are, and who you're around matters

Your surroundings, such as your home, school and place of work, where you spend most of your days, affect how you think, respond and behave. They should therefore reflect the high vibration you are trying to achieve within yourself and your life. Clutter is a conspiracy against clarity. That is my personal opinion, and I am sure many will agree with me. When our space is overwhelmed with clutter and just in a mess, this is often a reflection of a disorganised mind and has a feedback loop from feelings of chaos and confusion, which promotes procrastination, low self-esteem and confidence, anxiety and feelings of much lower vibrations. So, tidy up and de-clutter! Feel good about your space.

Hang around people and surroundings that are positive and inspiring. Not those energy vampires that suck your energy, leaving you deflated and defeated. Protect your energy; it is where your thoughts come from; it's your superpower.

Seek out the fear

It is common to default to so-called safety behaviours and actively avoid anxiety-inducing situations with social anxiety. Here are examples of some 'safety behaviours':

- When you feel anxious in a situation, you make an excuse to leave early, step outside, go to the bathroom to hide or pretend to be busy on your phone/fake a phone call.
- Zoning out or staring off into space and losing yourself in your thoughts to mentally escape the discomfort.
- If you're worried about sounding stupid or not making sense to others, you choose to speak as little as possible or not at all.
- Rehearsing conversation topics or practising what small talk you will make beforehand.
- Staying in the corners or spaces with fewer people around to avoid interactions or attracting attention from others.
- Pretending not to notice some people you know, maintaining distance, and avoiding eye contact to avoid meeting or running into them.
- Sometimes the response is so profoundly automated that you feel you have no control over your behaviours and go blank.

The following exercise requires you to spend some time identifying your safety behaviours. You will need to identify them so that you can erase them. Yes! Exchange your sabotaging safety behaviours with freedom. You will dance with your fears instead of avoiding them and trust me; you will realise that they weren't threatening at all.

Exercise 11: Avoidance out in the open

Observe how you feel and start noting down a list of whatever you do when you want to avoid or retreat from social situations. First, list all your fears, and then, taking each fear, write down the default safety behaviours.

Example:

FEAR:

"Using public transport makes me anxious."

SAFETY/AVOIDANCE BEHAVIOURS:

Staying inside.

Choosing not to run any errands even when you need to.

Making excuses not to go outside even when there is no alternative option for a ride.

Repeat with other fears and avoidance behaviours.

Do not rush this, as it's critical to the next step.

You will, from here on, follow the opposite action rule. One at a time, when you are faced with a daunting social situation that you are practically wired to avoid, you will do the opposite of what you're used to doing. You will be exploring the situation instead of avoiding it. Add the opposite action to all the avoidance behaviours you have listed for each fear.

OPPOSITE ACTION:

Visualise choosing to commute using public transport. Take a friend or family member along for moral support if needed.

Hey, you can do this. Start as slowly as you'd like; but do your best. Doing this exercise alone will take you closer to overcoming these fears that blocks you from moving freely and forward with your life. Take your time and be patient with yourself. By visualising the opposite action, you are teaching yourself what is possible and training your subconscious mind to see things differently.

So please close your eyes and dream of all the wonderful possibilities because they are endless. Allow yourself to let go and feel good. Remember that your mind doesn't know the difference between what it experiences for real and what it imagines with emotions. So, make it clear in your mind so you feel you have already done it for real when you open your eyes. If you can see and feel it with your mind, you can experience it for real and the best is

that it won't feel so scary after all. Keep visualising. Trust yourself.

Dancing with fear

Notice how you feel after the last exercise. Do you feel empowered or not too sure? Please write it down in your journal, as it's good to record your feelings as you go along. This record will show you how far you have come.

Now you have your list of social situations that make you anxious and what you do to avoid them. Next, let's move to Exercise 12, the second part of facing your fears.

Exercise 12: Let's dance

With your list of the things you avoid doing due to the discomfort of anxiety in doing them, e.g. going shopping, going for a walk by yourself, speaking to someone new, going to an event such as a party. Grade each activity on this list according to the level of anxiety you feel from least to most as you think about doing each of them.

Select the one that gives you the least anxiety to begin with.

Note down:

- The date,
- The activity,
- The predicted level of anxiety you think you will feel in doing the activity
- The prediction statements, which are the reasons why you think you cannot do it.

When you are ready, carry out the activity you have selected. You can continue visualising carrying out this activity to reduce the anxiety you feel in the actual situation. Tell yourself everything good is going to happen, and then go for it!

Once you have carried out the activity, note down what actually happened and how anxious you felt during and after it.

If you bailed the first time, it's ok, be kind to yourself. Give yourself a little time and space to process, then go for it again.

After successfully overcoming this activity once, "Hi five BTW!" Repeatedly do the activity until you feel very little to no anxiety. You are now ready to challenge yourself with the next least challenging activity on your list. Repeat the exercise for all the things on your list.

Example:

DATE:

10/09

ACTIVITY:

Asking my classmate for help with homework

PREDICTED ANXIETY RATINGS:

90%

PREDICTION STATEMENTS :

He's going to think I'm too dumb to figure it out myself.

He's going to tell everyone I can't do my own homework.

WHAT ACTUALLY HAPPENED :

He offered to revise lessons with me and help me catch up. He was nice to me and found me interesting.

ACTUAL ANXIETY LEVEL:

40%

Hang onto your list and challenge yourself regularly. Since you started with the lowest difficulty level and then proceeded to the highest, this is known as the gradual exposure technique. It will help you build your skills to tolerate the discomfort you feel while exposing your fears for what they really are, thoughts you made up in your mind.

For this CBT technique of exposure therapy to work, knowing the name and face of the triggers for the anxiety you feel is important. Confronting these fears, seeing them for what they truly are rather than running away from them, exposes them as nothing to fear. So you practice doing stuff outside the comfort of your subconscious programming on purpose, so you can grow and adapt safely and in a controlled manner. You learn to push through fears, teaching your body (subconscious mind) that the program needs changing as you are safe and there is nothing to be afraid of. In other words, changing your behaviour to train your mind to think differently, as the program it is running is irrational and redundant.

Welcoming people and allowing them the chance to welcome you

A general rule of thumb for making new friends is regularly showing up at a place where people meet. Showing up, being present, that's it. That's a small but massive step. You will soon grow comfortable in the environment, and before you know it, you won't mind the people so much either. Use the Exposure therapy method to get you ready for this if you are feeling too far out of your depth.

As this will be more of a long-term exercise, you can update an entry in your journal as often as you practice this.

Additionally, come up with a list of opportunities that will allow you to revisit social spaces and repeat encounters and interactions with other people.

Some ideas of social opportunities:

- Clubs at school
- Sports at school or local gyms and facilities
- Signing up for a swim team
- Classes or workshops (pottery, painting, cooking, etc.)
- Volunteering (nursing homes, hospitals, schools, charity organisations)
- Coffee shops or bookstores

You may also search online or ask acquaintances for any references or places that offer social opportunities. Again, override avoidance behaviours and allow fresh opportunities to build yourself an incredible, supportive social network. There are kind, like-minded people out there who would love to meet you as much as you would like to meet them. Do it, and you will see.

Start your day right: 'You got this!'

Setting the tone for your day as soon as you wake up is a vital part of your self-care routine. How you start your day determines the way the rest of your day will go. Start your day on a positive note. Start with your daily meditation, your affirmations, prayer, and or some breathing exercises. This will anchor you and ground you, align you and fortify you for anything the day throws at you. Most successful people start their day doing these things. Having a routine and regimen helps you feel more secure. Next, incorporate physical exercise into your morning routine. It can be as simple as doing 5-minute stretches or a quick yoga routine.

Spend extra time dressing well, doing your hair and getting ready in the morning. Looking good will surely help you feel good.

Music can be very therapeutic. It significantly impacts the mood. Happy music can uplift your mood, whereas sad music can slow you down or bum you out. While you're getting ready, put on something that has a high bpm (beats per minute) with lyrics that can inspire a hopeful, optimistic mood for the day and even help you feel more confident in yourself. Here are a few suggestions:

- Roar by Katy Perry
- Eye of The Tiger by Survivor
- Little Giant by Roo Panes
- Happy by Pharrel Williams

Why not create a playlist for yourself that empowers and inspires you?

Lastly, always keep in the back of your mind the image of your best self, strong, bold, confident, sociable, and always getting better and better.

Phew, what a workout! Great job on coming this far, but the work isn't done yet though. You know, progress is not linear. Sometimes, you might find yourself repeating old habits; you may feel defeated by negative thoughts or need time to recuperate from the social world. That's ok. Recognise that you are aware you are off course and notice where you went wrong and what you need to do to go right. Never beat yourself up. Look at how far you have come and remember the freedom you are living for. So get up, dust yourself off and go again. Remember, you have lots of exercises to turn to for support. You will succeed if you make better choices and allow yourself to stay open while repeating the exercises regularly. One day they will stick indefinitely.

> *Align your focus with the solution and not with the problem*
>
> — Unknown

Chapter 6
A wholesome life for positive change
Adjust your lifestyle

> *Mood is regulated by the brain, and to work properly, the brain needs optimal fuel from nutrients in food*
>
> — Dr Kaleigh McMordie

Diet: 'Eat right'

What you put in, you get out. The food that you eat should nourish you, help you develop, and stay energised, so you're prepared to deal with any obstacles that come your way. Some foods can indeed affect and contribute to a jittery mood, while others can help calm you and keep you strong mentally and physically. So let's see how healthy eating habits can make a world of difference in changing your lifestyle positively.

Research shows that a higher fruit and vegetable intake is associated with less perceived stress (Bagatini 2022). Additionally, An article in the BMJ, says that the food we eat plays a part in our moods. So, for your brain and body to function correctly, they require sufficient fuel and energy from the nutrients in your food. Your brain uses nutrients and amino acids derived from healthy food to make its neurotransmitters, such as serotonin and dopamine. These neurotransmitters have a huge responsibility in keeping your mental health status up to par.

Highly processed and refined foods are high in preservatives and artificial flavours and do not support a healthy mind and body; in fact, they do the opposite. Similarly, foods that are just pure sugar with no nutritional value are of no benefit to your mind and body. Eating whole foods is the way forward. Eat lots of fresh fruits and vegetables. Avoid genetically modified foods such as those containing gluten. Cut down on meat and drink plenty of water. Certain nutrients are crucial to healthy mind development and healing, such as:

Magnesium and omega-3 fatty acids. Deficiency in these nutrients has significant links with symptoms of anxiety and depression. So, let's quickly look at that to get an idea of what they are and why they matter. Keep in mind that these are not the only minerals the brain and body need. However, I want you to see a few examples of why eating well is important.

Magnesium

Minerals are one of the 4 groups of essential nutrients. The others are vitamins, essential fatty acids and amino acids. Minerals carry out important chemical reactions in your body and regulate electrical impulses in your brain.

Magnesium is one of the essential minerals important for improving your mood. Some sources of magnesium include:

- Vegetables like dark, leafy greens (spinach, kale)
- soybeans
- nuts and seeds
- Avocados
- Bananas
- legumes
- whole grains

Omega-3 fatty acid

Research on medical students showed that omega-3 fatty acid deficiency is linked with anxiety and depression (Kiecolt-Glaser 2011). Medical students must undergo a tonne of stress in their academic life and career and find a healthy balance between all other aspects of their life. When these students were provided with sufficient supplementation of omega-3, they showed a decrease in anxiety symptoms. Some sources of omega-3 fatty acids include:

- Cold-water fish (salmon, tuna, and mackerel).

- Nuts and seeds.
- Food cooked with or includes vegetable oils (canola oil, flaxseed oil).

Other nutrients suggested for optimal brain and body function are:

- Vitamin D (oily fish, milk, healthy amount of sun exposure)
- Folate (beans, peanuts, fresh fruits and juices)
- Micro-biotics (yoghurt, soft cheeses, sourdough bread, kefir water)

It is understandable if you do not have the time or money to care about the food you feed your brain and making sure its nutritional value is nothing less than perfect. In this case, multivitamin supplements are your best friend. Multivitamins can help supplement multiple vitamins and minerals your body utilises, helping curb deficiencies and put you back in balance. You can purchase quality multivitamins from the health food shops and start taking a course of those right away.

For a quality source of vitamins and minerals, I recommend Lily and Loaf, the company I have used for many years for myself and my family. I am also an affiliate, check them out:

https://lilyandloafinternational.com?aff=12026637

However, multivitamins must not be a substitute for a balanced meal, but the two may complement each other very well. ***Please consult your medical doctor or health professional for professional advice on any possible adverse effects BEFORE taking any supplements.***

Cut back on caffeine

Foods or drinks that contain caffeine, especially sodas and coffee, increase your heart rate, interfere with your circadian rhythm (when your mind starts to wind down and let your body know it's time to sleep) and make it difficult to fall asleep at night. They also cause shakiness, fidgeting and irritability. Does it sound similar to the symptoms of anything else you know of?

Sometimes, you may need to pull an all-nighter to catch up on homework and try to meet deadlines. I think we have all been there. But, it's a short-term solution and borderline self-harm because you neglect your sleep and the peace of your mind and body. It only guarantees a sleepless night combined with a caffeine crash, a recipe for disaster.

Watch your sugar intake

Your brain gets a massive surge of the feel-good chemical called dopamine after eating sugary foods. This feel-good rush is why sugar addiction is such an epidemic right now.

People use food to help them feel better or fill some emotional need.

Breast milk is the only natural food that combines fats and sugar as a meal. This milk is necessary for a new growing baby. However, even though we are no longer babies, when we feel emotionally challenged and want the feeling of safety and care, we regress to being babies and crave sugary and fatty foods.

Sure, you can enjoy something from a wrapper or a menu item from a fast food place every once in a while. However, bear in mind that the craving is for a reason, usually to fill an emotional void of some kind. Get conscious of what you are putting in your body and why. Eating lots of sugar, especially if you are inactive and not burning it off with exercise, will cause you to gain weight as the excess sugars get converted to fats and stored around your organs and beneath your body's skin. In addition, eating sugary food promotes a decline in your immune system, leaving your body inflamed and susceptible to infection and even cancer. You probably also notice the high or rush you get with refined sugar is swiftly followed by what has been termed the 'sugar crash', which leaves you feeling sluggish, lazy, sleepy, irritable, etc. The sugar industry is massive because people rely on the rush of dopamine to feel good, which is short-lived, so they crave more and more, spiralling into a very unhealthy place. It's technically a drug to the body, and like any drug comes with an array of adverse side effects. Ideally, cut out all sugary foods altogether, but if this is difficult, adopt the 80/20 rule of eating healthily. 20 percent of the time you can eat sugary snacks, if 80 percent of the time, you eat healthy foods.

Eating too little or too much

There is a complicated relationship between anxiety and hunger because both can exacerbate each other and can get confusing. What's going on? Are you anxious because you're feeling stressed, so therefore you cannot eat? Or are you eating too much because you are anxious?

Did you know that the mind and gut are connected? In fact, the gut is now widely known as the second brain. So if your gut health is poor, your mental health suffers too. Similarly, if your mental health is poor, the rest of your body can be stressed too. Consequently, the signs and symptoms of distress manifest physically, e.g. nausea, easily upset stomach, constant "funny feeling" in your tummy, diarrhoea or constipation and stomach aches.

Be mindful when you experience hunger or the lack of it. Anxiety can make you forget your body's needs, which is the fight-flight mechanism at play. For example, when a tiger is chasing you, you worry primarily about escaping from becoming dinner, not about what you will be having for dinner. Similarly, if you get so wrapped up in the stresses of your worries or your work, you might forget to have regular and healthy meals. Feeling embarrassed about eating and drinking is also a part of experiencing social anxiety, resulting in meal-skipping for many. Skipping meals causes hypoglycaemia, the scientific term for low blood sugar ('hypo-' as in less, 'glycaemia' meaning the presence of glucose in the blood). Symptoms of hypoglycaemia align with those of anxiety, such as irritability and nervousness. Hypoglycaemia also causes weakness, light-headedness and dizziness.

Overeating is the other end of the spectrum. Filling the void of hopelessness and fear with food for comfort. Unfortunately, comfort foods are not usually of a healthy, life-giving nature, as explained earlier. They are filled with sugar and fat, and as we are no longer infants, chronic intake of this will only mess up your gut and brain health.

So, listen to your body and ask yourself, "Am I hungry, or am I stressed and trying to fill an emotional void?" "What can I do right now to relieve my stress first?"

Bottom line, you are what you eat

The foods you put inside your body also have specific vibrational frequencies; therefore, to support vibrating at a higher frequency, eat foods of high vibration. Fresh foods filled with the nutrients needed to maintain high vibrations will leave you feeling alive, bright, vibrant, and healthy. So, the fresher it is, the more energising it is, reflecting positively on your body and energy field. Conversely, eating empty-calorie foods like potato chips, fries, or anything with an unnaturally long shelf life is not high-energy food; it's very poor in quality and unsustainable.

Physical exercise: 'Get up, move your body and energise

You are mostly energy; remember, we learned that in chapter 1. Your body is designed to move and be active, which is a requirement to replenish its energy store. It has an intricate design, built-in strength and resilience to temperatures, physical injury or trauma, an ability to climb mountains, walk long distances, lift things, fuel your incredible nervous system, and so much more. When you exercise, your heart beats faster to get the blood flowing to all body parts, so there's enough oxygen and nutrients for everything to function smoothly. As the energy levels in your body increase, the increase in blood flow and energy to your brain results in the release of endorphins (feel-good hormones) that can brighten up your mood. It reduces the levels of stress hormones such as cortisol and acts as a great quick fix for a low mood.

Exercise can instantly curb the vicious cycle of negative thinking. For example, when you get up and go on a brisk walk or do a quick workout, you can quickly get distracted from your negative thoughts and emotions. It is especially an active way of releasing tension in your mind and body that eventually relaxes you and improves your mood.

Science says that exercise reduces the intensity of your body's reaction to anxiety (Schoenfeld 2013), (Anderson 2013). Exercise exposes your body to physical sensations similar to those you experience when anxious, such as increased heart rate and rapid breathing. So, the more you exercise, the more you learn the same physical symptoms of anxiety as your tolerance for such physiological responses increases. You will also learn that these symptoms are responses of your body regulating itself and mostly there is nothing to fear.

In time with regular exercise, you will teach your body to remain calm even in challenging situations.

Not only does improving physical exercise make for an excellent coping skill, but it's also a phenomenal change that can boost the quality of your lifestyle. For example, it can play a role in creating your social support system if you're joining the gym or a sports team. Not to mention, it also improves your sleep quality.

While incorporating exercise into your lifestyle, remember to start with something you will enjoy. Exercise is meant to be an activity that gives you a thrill. It should give you something to look forward to, not dread. So, try out a bunch of options and find something you genuinely love that rejuvenates you.

Yoga

Yoga combines mental and physical exercises, including stretches and rhythmic breathing. I know all the poses can look a little too 'fancy' or complicated, but yoga is for everyone of all ages, and its primary goal is to gently ease past your body's resistance by letting go to feel relaxed and calm at the end of each session.

Some benefits of yoga include healthy brain development, improved concentration, better sleep quality, a noticeable reduction in stress (mentally and physically) and anxiety, greater flexibility and corrected posture.

Your psychological health is closely related to your posture as well. The psychological effects of posture improvement in students with health problems were assessed. The study reported incredible positive effects of postural intervention in those students, such as improved confidence, energy and reduced overall stress. Improving posture helped these students adjust better in school because their overall physical and mental health improved (Maekawa 2021).

Having a guide or instructor always helps reassure you when trying anything new. Try *"Yoga with Adriene"* on YouTube or the Daily Yoga phone app.

Aerobic exercise

Aerobic is a term that means "with oxygen," so aerobic exercise means you're using up a lot of oxygen while exercising;

the more you have to breathe and the faster your heart has to pump blood. Oxygen needs to reach all your muscles so they can work and strengthen while you exercise.

Although your heart rate is high while exercising for obvious reasons, cardio decreases your resting heart rate, which means how fast your heart beats when you aren't exerting yourself physically. As mentioned earlier, this aligns with the conclusion of research stating that exercise reduces the intensity of your body's reaction to anxiety.

Aerobic exercise is any physical activity that increases your heart rate and breathing, done continuously for some time, ideally 10 to 20 minutes or longer if you can.

Some examples are: running, jogging, swimming, bike riding, hiking and climbing stairs. Besides that, thanks to the internet, endless workout videos are available online. I would recommend *Fitness Blender's cardio or HIIT* workouts on YouTube.

Practice is not for perfection; it's for progress. Your subconscious mind has been running these anxiety programs for a while and will not take the change you are beginning to introduce lightly. This change is unfamiliar territory, and your subconscious thinks that because you are not good with the new and unknown, it must stop you, distract you, and redirect you till you return to the 'norm'. So, your motivation levels change throughout the week. After you come up with an exercise regimen, you might feel super motivated initially, but as time goes on, you might lose that motivation as your subconscious mind tries to get you back to the familiar, anxious and stressed because it believes you will be in danger of exposure if it doesn't.

Don't be disheartened if that happens; keep going. If you have tried and made an effort to start, you deserve a praise! Whoop whoop!! Keep practicing to teach your subconscious the changes you want it to adapt. If you get bored or tired, you could use some change, so try switching between different forms of physical exercise. If going on a long walk bores you, try putting on upbeat music in your room to dance to or copy moves from choreography videos. If you love nature and greenery, joining a hiking group might interest you. The options are endless. Since healthy lifestyle changes are personal and are meant to make you feel good, you can choose how you like to go about making them. You can even add empowering affirmations to overcome the subconscious pull, such as: ***Every day in every way I am getting stronger and stronger.***

Breathing

One of the top therapist-approved coping skills is… *drum roll please* …

Breathing!

You must be wondering, isn't breathing just another regular body function? You don't even have to think twice about doing it; your body just does it for you, to, you know, keep you alive.

However, in preparing for when anxiety strikes, when you feel like you don't know what to do, you need to learn proper breathing techniques.

So here's a handy little gadget to add to your toolkit that will help you across many points of overwhelming stress.

Breathing difficulties most commonly occur during panic attacks or anxiety attacks. However, they can also happen in any case of nervousness, such as severe social anxiety and moments where you are so stressed that your body holds tension in its muscles as you hold your breath.

Anxiety attacks and other stressful situations have identifiable triggers, such as:

- Feelings of being seen or judged
- Self-consciousness
- Remembering a time when you experienced similar feelings, i.e. felt sick from how anxious you were, tightness in your chest, etc
- Fear of having an anxiety attack at a wrong time and place
- Thinking you're going to fail
- Poor sleep and diet
- Having to show up someplace or speak where you'll attract attention from others

It can feel difficult to catch your breath during acute anxious episodes because your heart beats fast, and you don't breathe correctly to keep up with the demand. It can be a scary feeling. Remember, it's the fight or flight response that is subconsciously being activated to protect you. Your subconscious mind does not know the difference emotionally between what is real and what is imagined. You know a lion isn't chasing you; still, any anxiety-triggering event, such as a trip to the mall, walking down a busy road or giving a class presentation, is perceived as a threat and the body acts out accordingly. Hey, always keep in mind that the symptoms you feel are secondary to a primary cause, which is your thoughts and the pictures you create around those thoughts.

Before we even get into the breathing exercise, let's understand breathing better. If you want results, there are things you need to be clear about to do the exercise correctly.

> *"The more you can slow down the physical sensations during periods of high anxiety, the more you can use your rational mind to assess what is going on."*
>
> — Elke Kuercher-White

According to breathing coach Emma Ferris, 80% of people don't breathe properly as they don't use the total capacity of their lungs. Instead, they shallow-breathe using the upper part of their lungs and not the lower parts. So therefore, the diaphragm doesn't get fully extended, so they don't take in enough oxygen to get to all the organs and glands in the body. Breathing like this means only breathing enough to survive but not enough to thrive.

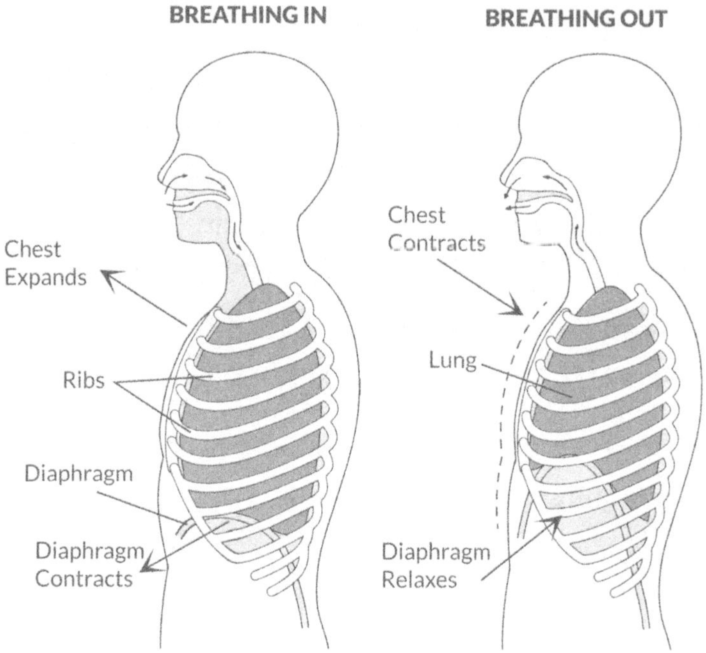

Diagram 6: *The mechanism of breathing*

Let's test whether you are breathing correctly now. Sit comfortably in an upright position; now observe your posture. Are you slumped forward with your shoulders rounded forward? Or are they back and relaxed? Your posture is the number one thing to address before taking on any breathing exercises. When your posture slumps, you curl the shoulders forward, lowering your lungs' capacity (See

Diagram 6); therefore, it's impossible to fully expand the lungs when you take a breath. Slumping means you can't fill your lungs entirely and, therefore, cannot fully oxygenate your body. Yes, you are alive, but some organs, such as your brain, heart and gut, have reduced energy. Think of where your heart resides in your body, between your lungs, under your ribcage and think of the added pressure on it when you slump or slouch over. So, your heart is under physical stress from poor posture and emotional stress from anxiety. So, sit and stand up straight and get relaxed.

Have you ever heard of the energy centres of your body? The Hindu tradition calls them Chakras. I won't go into any details about them, but here is a link to give you more information.

https://www.elitelearning.com/resource-center/rehabilitation-therapy/the-bodys-energy-centers/

To summarise, our bodies are wired via the nervous system. The brain is the central processing centre of the nervous system. The extension of the brain, the spinal cord, gives off bits of itself through the spine as spinal nerves that take light information along specific pathways to all our organs and glands for your bodily functions to occur. Information is also fed back to the brain via these spinal nerves along specific pathways to the brain to inform on what's happening in the body and how to respond. Seven energy centres of the body are established from the coming together of groups of nerves supplying the cells in different areas and levels of the body. The energy emitted from these collective groups of cells creates an energy centre.

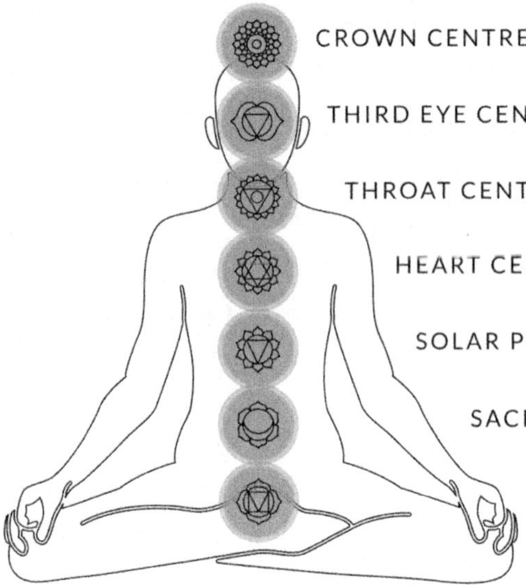

***Diagram** 7: Energy Centres/Chakras of the body*

> *In order to sustain life and health our cells communicate with each other by exchanging vital information transmitted on different frequencies of light*
>
> — Dr Joe Dispenza

When we don't breathe properly, the frequency of energy diminishes. When we turn on the stress response, we drain these centres of vital energy we need to thrive. This is why dysfunctions in the immune system, the gut and the heart are so closely linked to anxiety. Think about it: what do you feel when you are in a social situation? Yes, you feel anxious. What are the symptoms of anxiety? Does your heart race? Do you feel you can't breathe? Do you get clammy? Does your mind get scrambled? Do you get knots in your stomach? Do you feel nauseous? Do you get the picture? All these symptoms are responses the body makes because it feels it's not safe. It takes an awful lot of energy to support this. Imagine then this behaviour has been going on for a long time. Your energy centres will deplete, and more chronic issues will occur as there is insufficient energy for essential bodily functions.

One of the signs that your heart energy centre is struggling is that you suffer from social anxiety. Observe Diagram 7. Notice the position of the Heart centre.

> “*A blocked Heart Chakra side-lines self-confidence and self-esteem. We all get nervous once in a while, but what you feel is bigger. You feel inadequate around your friends or family, thinking that you won't ever measure up to them – their income, their marriages, their material things, their lives.*
>
> *In social settings, you feel you're being compared to others or judged by different standards. You might feel that you don't have anything constructive to offer to a conversation. These feelings lead to hesitation to*

communicate when around others. This interference also hinders your ability to make friends.

— The Heart Energy Activator

Clearing and energising this centre will help you to express yourselves and connect with others, including yourselves; you'll feel lighter in your spirit, less prone to negative emotions, empowered, and have a more positive outlook on life in general and in your relationships.

Breathing and thinking well, restores the life force of energy in your body's energy centres to create a healthy energy field around your body. When your energy field is strong, you feel safe, grounded, open to exploring, happy, and secure in yourself. It's simple really.

So roll your shoulders forward, then roll them up towards your ears, then roll them back, and let them drop down gently, squeezing the shoulder blades towards each other. Make sure your lower back is straight, with a gentle curve pointing forward. Sitting on the bony protrusion in your buttocks, not your sacrum or spine. Your head should not be projecting in front of your shoulders but should be directly on top of the shoulders. Simply, it feels like you are gently sticking your chest ahead of your head, leading with your heart but taking your head with you. Good posture is also essential when standing and walking around. This keeps all the energy centres open and supportive of each other.

Check your sitting posture: From the side as you sit, there should be a straight line from the hole of your ear to the centre of your shoulder to the hip bone as you sit. If you are sitting on a chair, keep your feet flat on the ground or the floor. Make sure your knees are not higher than your hips as you sit. If you are sitting on your bed or sofa, arrange your legs in the lotus position. This is an ideal sitting posture. In this optimal posture, you can now take a very deep breath.

Become aware of what happens to your body when you take each breath. For example, do your shoulders rise up, or does your belly expand? Of course, what you want is for your belly to expand and your shoulders to remain where they are in a nice, relaxed position. If you're finding it difficult getting your belly to expand, then you will need to practise some more, filling up your lungs correctly using the diaphragm. Once you've mastered this, you can move on to the breathing exercise.

Your body is yours to take care of, and it will take care of you. So let's do some deep breathing.

Exercise 13: Breathe to thrive

Find a comfortable position and become present with your physical body. Wiggle your toes, rub your hands

together, relax your jaw, neck and shoulder muscles, and think: "I am okay. I am safe."

Close your eyes.

- On a count of 1 and 2, breathe slowly and deeply in through the nose, letting the air fill up your lungs as your abdomen expands.
- Hold on a count of 3 and 4.
- As you exhale on 5 and 6, think to yourself:

"I am doing my best, and that is good enough."

Again, Breathe deeply in on 1 and 2, hold 3 and 4, and as you breathe out 5 and 6, think:

"I can always do better, and I will."

With each exhale, let your body relax while you think of these statements and direct them to yourself. Replace any negative, self-critical thoughts with new positive ones.

With every inhale, welcome this positive energy. Let every breath speak to you in your mind and in your heart. Let it encourage and empower you. Know that you are fully capable of being a bright and accomplished person.

Now, focus your breath into your chest, the area of your heart's energy centre, continuing to let go of any tension in this area as you exhale. Spend some time here while

allowing gratitude and love to lighten this area and rebalance this centre.

Do this exercise for 5 mins or more, 3 times per day or more. Again, focus on your breath as you repeat the statements.

Sleep: 'Charge your battery'

8-10 hours is the recommended amount of sleep on average for teenagers 14 to 17 years. Less than 8 hours of sleep causes symptoms characteristic of anxiety. Sleep and rest are basic needs that should not be compromised.

Sleep reduces stress, improves mood, helps you think more clearly and helps you do well academically because it optimises brain functions.

'Is it really so bad if I don't get all 8 hours of sleep?'

Sleep supports the brain in replenishing itself by removing toxins and regenerating brain cells, making the nervous system and the body refreshed, rested, rejuvenated and ready for functioning the following day. Anxiety is one of the top problems brought on by a lack of sleep. A study proved that sleep deprivation brings unwanted, negative moods (Babson 2010). If you don't get at least 8 hours of sleep at night, your efforts during the day may be wasted. In the short term, a lack of sleep can impair your ability to think clearly and process information smoothly. It can leave you moody and less able to get up or even attempt the things you need to do, and whatever you manage to get done will likely lack your best results.

Sleep better suggestions

- Take the matter of getting enough sleep seriously and prioritise it.
- Turn off your screens at the same time every day when going to bed, at least an hour before. Using your phone before bed, as most do, does not allow your mind to wind down and relax the way it needs to while trying to put you to sleep. It actually keeps you alert, which is not conducive to sleeping. This is because you are not allowing your mind to wind down from Beta, to Alpha, to Theta and Delta brain waves where deep restful sleep is found (See Diagram 5, Chapter 4). So, put your phone on 'Do not disturb' mode and leave it across the room, away from your bed, and out of your reach if necessary.
- Try reading a book if you can't fall asleep at night instead of unlocking your phone. The light on your phone is a stimulus to keep you awake.
- Listen to your body; when you feel sleepy, hit the pillow.
- Start your day with a healthy habit. Keep a glass of water by your bed to drink in the morning as you

wake up instead of reaching for your phone. Get up and do some stretches to wake up your body, wash up first and get dressed or map out your day in your mind in a positive way.

- If you have difficulty sleeping which is making the anxiety worse, you may benefit from listening to something relaxing since it'll take your mind off things. If you don't have Google or Alexa to ask, there's a small allowance to access your phone here just to put something on in the background. People listen to whale sounds, white noise, ambient noise such as that of an aeroplane cabin or the hum of a fan or AC, meditation exercises or even rain sounds, anything that can lull them to sleep. Do what works for you.
- Cut down stress. Stress will make it more difficult to fall asleep. Do you ever go to bed on time but end up lying awake for a long time with a racing mind rather than falling asleep? To counter the stress response, do what relaxes you. Breathing, meditation, use one of the many exercises you have in this book to help you.

The bottom line is, if you aren't getting enough sleep at night, you should be!

Think better of yourself, feel better about yourself

Get conscious and deliberate about cleaning up your thoughts and the power you have when using them. Use words wisely because when you speak, your thoughts create feelings, which create your vibes/energy, which attracts similar energy to you. Energy attracts energy.

More blatantly put, negative energy is matched with negative energy and brought back to you as some experience of similar frequency. Positive energy works precisely the same. Simply put, if your vibes are negative, you will receive negative vibes in return. If however, your vibes are positive, good things are headed your way.

So, what are the things you say and feel about yourself when you feel anxious?

Is it negative and defeating? No wonder you feel rubbish. Your mind, being as clever as it is, guides you to what you focus on the most. It is up to you to control your focus. Focus on what you want ONLY, not what you don't want.

Social media: 'Connection or addiction?'

How are you using social media or is social media using you? What is its purpose to you? These are essential questions to ask yourself and think about in this section.

Do you reach for your phone as soon as you wake up? Ah, there are far too many reasons why you should not do that.

If you want to make small changes, start here: Don't use your phone as soon as you wake up.

Phone usage and sleep

When you wake up, your brain transitions from Delta waves (produced in deep sleep) to Theta waves (waking up/half asleep state). Then, your brain shifts to Alpha waves, where you are awake, relaxed, and haven't begun processing much information yet. When you hop onto social media apps as soon as you wake up, you don't allow your brain to take the time it needs to wake up. Your brain is forced to skip the necessary Theta and Alpha waves stages and jump straight from the Delta stage (deep sleep) to the Beta state (wide awake). The Theta state is significant because that is also the perfect time to check in with your subconscious mind, envision your goals and decide the next best actions to help you achieve what you want. So, consuming content right after waking up robs your brain of operating at its best.

Media Inundation

Aside from how you use social media, the social media content you consume and how much time you spend on it has a significant impact. For example, if you are following the news, you'll come across it mostly during your scrolling time. A mind constantly buzzed with the news on the declining climate change status or reports of ongoing wars, shootings and murders may leave you shaken and feeling unease and dread, disrupting your energy field with thoughts of low vibrations and worry. On the other note, if you follow pop culture, entertainment and the lives of other famous people, you may be distracting yourself from your own life and not reaping any benefits, gaining any knowledge, or helping yourself grow.

There is much more to be concerned with besides the lives of other people, such as your own life. Distractions are okay. Sometimes you need to be distracted from a negative mood or overwhelming emotions during or after 'a lousy day'. You may go online and scroll through content to engage in doing anything to take your mind off things. The problem is the length of time spent and distracting yourself is neglecting your goals and dreams as you focus on things that won't necessarily help you. Besides, as you scroll through other people's lives and achievements, you inevitably compare yourself to them. You deserve better than that. Listen my friend; if it's not inspiring you to get up and be a better person, change is needed. If, on the other hand, you are being encouraged to be your best self, carry on and stay focused in that direction.

Limiting your usage

Your online identity isn't all you are. You must be able to step away from your phone and see what defines your world and you as a person. Your interests, preferences, hobbies, habits, lifestyle, skills and the people in your life reflect your true character and general make-up, not the filtered photos and captions, and especially not the number of likes and comments you get under what you upload online.

You have total control over what you choose to do on your phones and what kind of content you follow and interact with. So it is totally up to you to use social media effectively, to be more productive and better informed.

Granted, there is so much well-curated and exciting online content on social media that it shouldn't be all classed as bad. Professional dancers, health gurus, phenomenal artwork; the online stream of content is endless. Who wouldn't want to see what's out there? But is it worth letting social media overwhelm your time, commitments and your life? Unhealthy, excess social media usage is easily the root cause of many problems, and many users have fallen victim to its addictive interface. It was designed this way. People and algorithms are targeting you to keep you hooked for profit while your life goes to shambles. Take your power back! The overstimulation provided by social media and the media lowers your ability to think originally and use your mind in the diverse way in which it is designed to be used. Social media misuse also forces you to rely on others to validate you (Granic 2020).

It is safe to say the online world isn't going anywhere anytime soon, so you won't miss out by logging off for a while. I am not anti-social media in any way as I use it quite a lot too. Just be careful not to get completely sucked up by it. Consider limiting your social media usage by doing something to eliminate the primary distraction. Here are a few tips:

- **Distance:** Create distance between you and the social media app's accessibility. Make it harder to open the app so that you remove the ease of accessibility factor. You can keep the app uninstalled and reinstall it to use it for a limited amount of time.
- **App locks and timers:** There are apps you can install to lock other apps on your phone, which prevents you from opening them. I recommend 'BlockSite-Stay Focused', which, as the name suggests, helps you focus on your tasks by preventing you from opening an app for a set period of time, e.g. block your social media app for 2 hours when you have to study or need some quality time for yourself.
- **Try phone-free, mindful eating:** Put your phone away when it's time to eat a meal or snack. We aren't mediaeval royalty that needs live entertainment from court jesters to watch while we eat. Mindful eating is one of the many recommended mindful exercises. Observe and watch your food; focus on each bite you take, the food's texture, taste, and what it smells like, chew each bite slowly and take in every other detail that you can. You'll naturally be eating something healthy, won't you?

Being social with a purpose

"You gotta put yourself out there!" is the annoying advice frequently thrown at those suffering from social anxiety. It's like telling someone suffering from pain that their pain isn't real.

Social anxiety, at its core, is the inability to "just put yourself out there" without being fueled by absolute crippling fear. On that note, some might even say, "What's there to be scared about? Don't worry; these people won't bite!" No, they don't bite. But they do talk. It scares you to wonder if they might be talking about you, judging you, your clothes, the way you are, and your entire existence. That's social anxiety. The first and most direct way to heal and be free from social anxiety is to realise that most times the judgment you think is coming from people is not real. Your perception makes it real to your mind, but it is you who are overthinking these things. Yes, I have said it before, and I'll repeat it until you get it; you are the object of your demise. I know you hate to hear that, but it's the best place to start, and you can start freeing yourself once you see, understand and accept this. Later on, in Chapter 7, you will learn about 'Self-love', which is the key to believing in yourself. That aside, to build your confidence skills, you must be willing to face embarrassment a few times. But don't look at it as 'embarrassment' but as 'learning'. You can't ice skate on the first go without falling a few times. It takes learning and practice to get better. Once you start building a healthier relationship with yourself, falling over and making mistakes won't bother you as you'll embrace them as learning and growing. Soon enough, you won't care what others think, but you will be focused on being true to yourself.

> *The path to FAILURE and the path to your FREEDOM are the same, the outcomes only differ because you resisted the unknown and fear kept you stuck OR you danced with the fear till it was worn out while the unknown became known, setting yourself free to explore life the way you deserve.*
>
> — ThashnaWalsh

You will always hear advice about joining more clubs, being active where there are more people, or chatting with groups. But that doesn't help, does it? It's hard because that could be precisely what makes you anxious, and as someone with social anxiety, you avoid situations and things that make you anxious. That is why you start slow. You might treat this as uncharted territory at first if it's your first time, but by practising and staying positive, it gets more accessible, and you will win.

So how do you make friends when you have social anxiety that keeps getting in the way?

You know what you like and what you're interested in best. Everyone has a taste for something, be it books, TV shows, chess, board games, music, film, cooking or playing sports. Find people that share your interests to bond and connect with, for example, a book club if you love reading. You will feel much more comfortable being around people with whom you have something in common. Remember how everything got digitally optimised when COVID popped up? I mean everything, especially ways for people to connect and talk online. You can find online clubs and meetings of interest that take place over video or audio calls if you aren't up for stepping out of the house. Try searching! Also, say yes to being invited to social events. You were invited, which means you are wanted there, so show up. It's an opportunity to overcome anxiety while socialising. You won't meet anyone or find someone to talk to sitting at home alone. So, be bold, and say yes! You will feel glad you did. You have got tools to help now, so no more excuses.

If you want to go to a social event or step into a social setting, but you find yourself feeling too anxious, use the Exposure technique from Chapter 5 to boss any avoidance behaviour and expose the fear. You can also bring along someone you trust. It will give you peace of mind knowing that someone is there to have your back. They can also help you start or carry on conversations with others if you need support. For example, they can help you speak to the retail assistant at the mall or order at the restaurant for you.

Make eye contact with whoever you speak with. Make yourself do it, remembering to breathe. Look at the colour of their eyes and their facial expressions. Hear what they are saying, stay present with the person. You don't have to stare into their souls or anything. Practice looking at them while they're talking, and smile or show you are listening attentively. You will get what you give out in return, so give out a positive presence.

You can be the one to ask questions and engage someone; they will appreciate it and return the same energy to you. Again remember, the majority of the people around you are feeling just as vulnerable. You don't have to design an entire conversation. You can say the simplest of "Hello! Good morning," "Good evening!" or ask, "How's your day going?" or "What do you like doing in your free time?" and it will have a good impression because people love to talk about themselves and love to feel heard. Also, them talking about themselves will give you time to breathe and not feel a need to perform. You will simply be settling in and connecting with another person.

Many people with social anxiety will revisit the interaction they have had after it is over. You might walk through every single thing you said or asked, every way you sat or stood, the way you nodded your head or laughed, etc. The longer those thoughts run, the more likely things will take a negative turn. Prevent overthinking with your favourite coping tool. Your breathing exercise!' (Exercise 13, Chater 6). Breathe and change your thoughts. Choose more constructive, inspiring thoughts. Commend yourself on stepping up to the plate of your life of freedom. Deep breath in, breathe out and let go. You're okay, and you did great back there.

Take your time on your journey to freedom. The goal is to keep moving, no matter how slow or little the steps are. Say hello to the shopkeeper, help someone in need, give others a hand, accept invites and accept people as they are - the same as you'd like to be accepted for who you are.

Try new things and take baby steps through fear to freedom. Know that you're well-equipped, young padawan. You have brilliant coping skills and extraordinary coping skills; you have phenomenal coping skills. Trust this.

You'll start seeing new light never seen before. You'll learn how lovely people can be, how everyone has a story to tell, how interesting other people's interests are, and that many people out there would love to know you. We all have something unique to pass along to another person, so, open your heart to find your way to where you belong, share your message, and grow into the human you want to be.

Chapter 7
Rewire and fire
Banish Social Anxiety

> *Live less out of habit and more out of INTENT*
>
> — Unknown

Let's now look at how to rewire your mind and banish social anxiety. Yes, for good. When you get the concepts and give yourself the benefit of any doubts you may have, together with perseverance, you will rid yourself of the crippling nature in which you are affected by social anxiety.

Healthily connect with yourself and disconnect from anxiety. Then you can work on building better habits while rewiring your brain, so it works for you and not against you. Good habits will define your life. Social anxiety, after all, is due to specific events and or a series of repeated bad habits developed over time.

Please put your fears aside and think about what I'm suggesting.

You may have already read some of the things here; why do I repeat them? Well, for starters, your mind learns by repetition. Another reason is that it is also imperative to the results of this chapter. So pay even closer attention if you have heard it all before because therein lies the answers you seek. Here we go.

Make a habit of trying new things, talking to new people, going out to new places, saying "yes" to plans more, and any other chance you get at gaining experience. That's right. When you expose yourself to the very thing that scares you, you take away your fear's control. You grow through what you go through. You learn so much about yourself when you allow yourself to experience more things. Get to know yourself.

Start by giving your brain more credit. It is where anxiety and uncertainty arise and affect how you view yourself and the world. You created the fear inside your mind that keeps you from trying new things. See how powerful you are? Well, that power goes both ways. Your brain is capable of changing itself profoundly, so give your mind an upgrade of fresh new thoughts and habits.

Let's talk about some of the science of habits in the brain to give you a sense of direction. I want to help you better understand how your brain works. We covered a lot of the basics in chapter one, so going back and reviewing is not a bad idea but not necessary. When you learn how a machine works, you know better when and how to use it. When you have learned how to use it, you have all the confidence you need to control it.

The brain creates habits, so it doesn't have to think too hard about doing things such as walking, talking, writing and so on, as it does it unconsciously. For example, ever pick up your phone automatically and open Instagram, not even realising you did it, especially when you should be studying or doing something important. Before you know it, you are scrolling, and oh no, two hours later! That's a habit you created, and you acted automatically. How does your brain do that?

First, you have a thought, 'I have to study for my test'. this thought is not one of pleasure, your heart flips as you realise you only have one day to study and it's a subject you despise. Your subconscious mind feels you and wants to steer you toward pleasure and away from the pain of studying. It says "Hey, it's time to pull out that old habit of yours that gives you a sense of self-satisfaction and safety".

Second, the habit itself, 'something you enjoy doing', the subconscious response to the thought with action. In this case, scrolling on your phone without a second thought. You scroll and you create posts, you comment on friends pics, you watch endless videos, and you feel hooked. Hours have passed as you try to push studying far away by distracting yourself scrolling. This is making you anxious because you know that if you don't start studying soon you are going to fail the class. Your mind turns up the pleasure volume and gives you another brilliant idea. "Why don't we go play a video game". "You can get lost in pleasure there and not have to think about studying and failing and all that awful stuff".

Lastly, the reward, the feel-good factor, helps the brain decide if the outcome felt good enough to repeat in the future. Yes, it does feel good getting lost in your phone or a video game and not having to face the discomfort of studying. If it works your brain will make a note to continue to do it in the future. Even though you know you have less time to study, if your willpower is not strong enough, studying will lose. Every time you get nervous, or you feel threatened you may retreat and scroll through your phone some more to block out what you fear or perceive as pain. Why are you doing this?

Located at the base of your brain is a centre called the basal ganglia. The basal ganglia are where habits are formed and stored. (Baladron 2020) It has connections running to all parts of the brain through a network of brain circuits. The more often you repeat a thought or action, the stronger those connections get until the action becomes automatic, unconscious or subconscious (they are all the same thing). When the connections are this strong, you don't think twice before doing that action. Unfortunately, your subconscious brain cannot distinguish between good and bad habits, making it challenging to change any bad habits.

You are likely consciously aware of your bad habits and know they limit you. Despite that awareness, trying to quit these habits is not a simple act. It takes a great deal of conscious effort, requiring enormous energy. From chapter one, you will remember that only 5% of the brain uses conscious efforts, while the rest is controlled subconsciously. As you have also learned before, using willpower to break a bad habit such as social anxiety would be like using a computer with a 40-bit processor to manage the job of a 40 million-bit processor. It is a slow, long and painful journey. It's not impossible though; let's look at some ways that you can adopt to make the journey easier.

The solutions

Calm your mind, still your energy:

Learn how to calm your mind. When you learn to stay calm, you rewire the parts of your brain that generate anxiety. When you're used to remaining calm, there is less noise in your head, you can think clearly and make better decisions.

Make breathing properly a habit. Go back to chapter 6. It is super important for a healthy mind. Go on, re-read it till you are entirely sure you have it, then do the exercises over and over to get the action memorised inside your body to become automated. This is the first step to calming your mind.

Focus on what you want more of:

You can train your brain to spend less time scrolling on Instagram, to eat healthier every day, to put your phone and laptop away before you go to sleep, to speak kinder to yourself, and not to self-deprecate when you mess up and so much more. You only have to choose to kick these limiting habits to the curb and decide that enough is enough - it's time to do some maintenance and rewire your brain.

When you repeat actions, your brain strengthens the connections responsible for carrying that action out. So, work to build better thinking habits of all the things you want to achieve. What does that look like? What does it feel like? Positive thoughts generate good energy and attract similar energy and actions, making life feel effortless and fun. If you slip back into negative focus, i.e. focusing on what you don't want, be aware and stop. Take a breath and say, "change!" Then, get back to a productive and socially positive thought.

Pay attention to the trigger and reframe it:

Watch closely for what triggers your negative response to social situations and lean into it. Observe it so you can recognise it the next time it pops up in the future. With this knowledge, you can develop a greater sense of self-control to master your mind instead of allowing it to control you. You can erase the bad and the ugly from your mind and bring in what's good for you. Bring in what frees you from social anxiety, not what cripples you. Replace your doubts about your abilities with faith in your strengths.

Big yourself up every time:

Adopt positive self-talk. Revisit chapter 4 and repeat daily affirmations until you believe you are capable, gorgeous, fun, smart, open, and full of love. You are unique, and there are many people wanting to get to know you; they love you. I mean, what's not to love? People who love themselves allow themselves to be loved and are also kind and loving to others. You want to surround yourself with this energy. How do you do that? You become loving to yourself, praise yourself and see yourself in a positive light. Big up yourself first; this permits others to do the same. It is not some egotistic thing, but a deep intrinsic appreciation for the beautiful creation that is you, unique, like the stars of the universe. Yes, the Divine intelligence that created you also created all the remarkable wonders of the universe; how could you possibly be flawed? You are perfect as you are. So, praise your awesome self.

Exercise 14: Strength to strength

Let's do a quick exercise to put things into perspective. Draw two columns on a page in your journal, one titled "My strengths" and the other "My weaknesses".

Ok, now cross through the word 'weaknesses' and above it write 'things I need to work on'. I deliberately did this because weaknesses are inhibiting. It's a negative word that does not inspire betterment but dismisses you into failure. Weakness is a choice. You can get strong at anything should you desire it.

In the 'strengths' column, list things you're good at or that you feel are good about you, from knowing how to cook good pasta to being a great listener and making your friends laugh.

In the 'things I need to work on' column, list things you think you want to work on. For example, maybe you need to drink less coffee, use social media less or avoid going to bed too late. Maybe you need to stop allowing people to take advantage of you. Perhaps you need to learn to speak up when something is bothering you. Exercise more maybe? This list will help you set goals and figure out what good habits you can work on building and what behaviours need disabling.

Now take each of the things you listed in the strengths column, close your eyes and describe how it feels to have this strength. Write this down in your journal. Let the feelings build as you revel in the energy of these feelings.

Some of these strengths may have come naturally to you; express gratitude for this, as someone somewhere has this in the list of things they want to improve on. Let pride well up inside you as you smile with gratitude that you are a natural at this.

You have had to work on some things in the 'strengths' list to get stronger at them. Become aware of what they are. You did what was necessary to become the boss of this, and this should make you feel proud. Write down everything you feel when you think about this achievement and how it happened. You may think to yourself. I am strong and resilient. I get what I want because I persevere. Write down some of the things you had to do to develop this strength. Maybe you wrote gratitude lists daily to keep you focused on the positives and keep your energy levels high.

Cool, now you know you are perfectly capable of making anything into a strength. "Fist bump!"

Now, in the list of things you need to work on, for each item, list what you need to do to accomplish each goal. What actions do you need to take to make these things happen? Then, feel what it will feel like once you have achieved it. Don't stop till you feel it and it makes you smile.

Next, take each thing you need to work on and do the actions to gain another strength. Practice for progress! Look at you growing from strength to strength.

No effort is discounted. Change is inevitable once you are doing the exercises. So have faith in yourself and the work and time you put into rewiring your brain, making better connections and reinforcing them with these exercises.

Have fun building new habits, however, be mindful of falling back into old patterns and routines, which can happen all too easily and is very common and can be very frustrating. Stay focused and strong.

Annihilate fear and self-doubt

Self-doubt is not trusting ourselves or our decisions and feeling unsure. You may find it difficult to make a decision because you're perpetually scared of making the wrong choice. Self-doubt stops you moving forward or forces you to put the control into the hands of someone else to make your decisions for you. When you're holding up the line at the cashier in the food court because you can't decide if you want the chicken or beef, that's self-doubt. When you ask your friend to do something you could do yourself, but you are too scared of judgement or that you may not say it right, that's self-doubt. When you have a cool outfit you never wear because you are afraid others won't like it as you do, that's self-doubt.

When you doubt yourself, you rob yourself of your life. Your goals, your ambitions, your fun and that of those you care about will be reflected in the liberation from this self-limitation. Fear of failure drives self-doubt, which drives social anxiety. When you close up because you are afraid of being vulnerable or open to making mistakes, you are fueling fear. When you're so scared of embarrassing yourself or possibly facing rejection, so you never try, fear has won. When you doubt your abilities and never give yourself the chance to see what is truly possible, not what your scared mind tells you is going to potentially happen, you are fueling fear. Continuing to fuel fear like this makes the fear and self-doubt grow stronger and more dominant. You are wiring your subconscious mind to hold on to this behaviour.

However, as we discussed throughout this entire book, to stay a slave to fear is really the biggest failure of all. You must walk through the fear; in other words, you must do the thing you fear to realise your potential, rewire your subconscious mind and grow to believe in yourself. If you never do this, you will not have the successful life of freedom you deserve. This applies to anyone, rich or poor, black or white, tall or short, fat or thin. Self-belief is the key to your life being a success. To face self-doubt, you have to practice dismissing it and embracing self belief. Imagine I gave you the manual on operating a forklift and told you what you need to know to use it. When I give you the keys to it, all you will know is the theory behind how a forklift works, but you won't be able to work it. That's the difference between theoretical learning and practice. So you will need to practice, practice, practice!

Remember the Exposure exercise in chapter 5. This will help you rewire fear as an aid to get you to a stronger, wiser, freer you, taking back your power.

Transforming the discomfort

Discomfort in social situations means that something feels new and unknown, and in those moments, your thoughts can make it scary, or they can make it exciting. Start conditioning yourself to know when the discomfort really is excitement confused by fear. Not all discomfort indicates a real threat. In fact, if you change the thought around it, you will soon find it to be very exciting and guiding you to your stronger self.

The discomfort of anxiety and the buzz of excitement are both arousal states of mind (they both excite your mind), so it's easy to get from one to the other. Anxiety is created from a story of resisting a perceived outcome, while excitement is created from a story welcoming the perceived outcome. The chemicals released to express these emotions in your body are practically the same, so the physiological reactions are also practically the same. So, your heart races, your pupils dilate, your respiration increases, your palms get sweaty, etc.

What sets anxiety and excitement apart is what you are thinking about, i.e. the story you are telling yourself, so the secret is changing your mindset to see an opportunity where you would usually see a threat. In other words, swap the story of anxiety or discomfort with one of excitement.

Making this switch is especially useful when you need to keep your energy high, such as when you are presenting to the class. For example, studies have shown that when public speaking triggers anxiety, attempting to calm yourself before the speech leads to poor performance, as the leap from high arousal state to a calm state is too great. However, staying in the same elevated state but switching from anxiety to excitement improved performance. (Brooks 2013).

Using the technique called Anxiety Reappraisal can be powerful for switching states if done well. It's probably the simplest of exercises. Ready? Here we go.

Exercise 15: Anxiety Reappraisal

So, the day for your presentation has finally arrived, and you have been practising, but you are completely freaking out about going on stage in front of everyone. You worry about all the what-ifs. You are shaking and can't seem to calm yourself down. You keep saying to yourself, "Oh my god, I'm freaking out!".

Instead of saying to yourself, "I am so nervous", "I'm freaking out!" or "I'm terrified!" swap those thoughts for "I am excited!", "I'm so excited!", "This is so exciting!", "What an exciting opportunity!", "I feel so much excitement right now!", "I am bursting with excitement!". Do you get the picture? Keep repeating this over and over and over again, feeling excited!

Think about the potential positive outcome.

Finally, GET EXCITED!

The repetition changes your subconscious mind and the belief and behaviours

---

> *Fear is excitement without breath*
>
> — Anonymous

Mindfulness

How to look and feel within yourself

Mindfulness is noticing what you're feeling by being present, and noticing it without judgement. It's accepting yourself as you are, regardless of the sensations or emotions arising within you.

Mindfulness lets you separate yourself from stressful tasks and supports mental well-being by giving you an easy way to neutralise negative emotions to restore your energy.

You can practice mindfulness techniques anywhere and at any time. Some well-known methods include breathing exercises, observing, body scanning and meditating. We covered meditation and breathing in chapters 4 and 6, respectively. Let's now do a simple exercise in body scanning that is quick yet effective in calming your mind and releasing anxiety. Body scan meditation can be practised while sitting at your desk or anywhere you won't be disturbed or while lying in bed before going to sleep.

Exercise 16: Body scan

Sit comfortably. Take a deep breath in through your nose and close your eyes as you breathe out through your mouth. Repeat 3 times.

Your eyes will remain closed as your mind begins to open up. Continue breathing deeply, knock at your mind's door and ask it to pay attention to your body's sensations. Notice what you're feeling in your body right now.

Start at the top of the head by becoming aware of your scalp, cars, forehead and face. Next, check in with your

breathing. Remember to breathe deeply in through your nose and out through your mouth.

Gently move your imaginary body scanners lower down through your body. Notice where you feel ease and comfort and where you feel discomfort or tightness. Take a deep, long, cleansing breath into each of these areas and say to yourself, "I know how this part feels, and it's okay." Breathe as you continue scanning.

Notice how your neck feels, notice how your shoulders, arms, chest, back and tummy also feel. Breathe through each part repeating, "I know how this part feels, and it's okay." and let go.

Feel your weight in your pelvic area, hips and legs while sitting there. What are you sensing? Notice how your body is resting on the surface you are sitting on and how it feels. Breathe and let go.

You don't need to change anything; only observe. So gently knock at the door of each part of your body, checking in to see how you're doing.

When you have checked all parts, be aware of your entire body and how it feels. Breathe in and repeat, "I am alive, and I am grateful." Then, breathe out and let go.

And there we go, a new tool for your toolkit. Remember to use it! Where you place your attention, you put your energy. So being mindful within helps to focus energy within your body.

Besides the body scan exercises, you can also practise mindfulness by simply paying attention to your surroundings by engaging all 5 of your senses (sight, smell, sound, taste, touch). Then, take 5 or 10 minutes to create a lasting sense of calm to get you through the rest of the day by practising this exercise with slow, rhythmic breathing, releasing and relaxing your muscles as you go along.

Self-love

Self-esteem is everything

Low self-esteem is the foundation of anxiety and low mood. When you love yourself, there is no way you would let yourself get stuck in a place of limitation. Self-love is empowering and inspiring. It causes you to rise above the odds, seek out your most vital and best self, and become it. You have picked up this book and are continuing to read because of self-love.

Self-love focuses on looking at yourself and accepting what you see: a person with the potential to accomplish so much and to live their best life. Self-love drives your desires and dreams. Self-love wants you to feel excited about life every day and thrive. Self-love will never give up on you.

We were all born with self-love, high self-esteem and confidence. However, life and its circumstances can easily distract us from the path of deep love and respect for ourselves. This distraction can leave us feeling unworthy, unloved and not good enough; we may even feel that good things are not available to us and that we are different, so no one wants to connect with us.

The good news is that these limiting thoughts are just that, thoughts.

It's time to erase these thoughts about you that hold no truth to them unless of course, you can absolutely prove that they do. And I can bet you that regardless of what you think about yourself, when the truth is uncovered, you'll find that you are loveable, worthy and full of amazing potential. You only need to extract the lessons from the experiences you have had and move on with just the truth.

Remember we spoke earlier about the subconscious mind and the beliefs we hold? Beliefs such as "I don't have what it takes to be likeable and make friends" or "I can't control this anxiety around other people, so I can't be with them." We spoke of these beliefs being self-limiting and that they are also feeding anxiety.

Your self-worth comes from within you. So, check for your inner voice and see what it says. Does it accept you and tell you that you are good, or does it say harsh things to belittle you? Does your inner voice make you think you aren't good enough? If your answer is the latter, chances are you're highly self-critical, as most people with social anxiety are. Now it's time to challenge that harsh inner voice. You won't be fighting yourself, but you will learn to connect with and love yourself and have a conversation with your heart.

Listen to your inner voice closely. Acknowledge it with no judgement when it starts to become critical of you. Tell yourself that you are alright and that you understand the pain, and you no longer need to hold on to it and anything it says. Look in the mirror, state your name and smile as you naturally do. Smiling with yourself helps you to feel better and uplifts your mood. Smiling with yourself reassures your mind that you (your name) are good. It's YOU, showing yourself compassion, and that is self-love.

Go on, get up, go to the mirror, find a mirror. Look and the beautiful being looking back at you. Say "hi (your name)" and smile.

When it comes to self-love, treat yourself the way you would treat someone you love deeply. Imagine yourself when you were younger, a child with their whole life ahead. What would you say to that child? Wouldn't you treat them gently? Then, learn to use that same gentleness for yourself.

Exercise 17: THINK

Stop and think about yourself. How you look, how you sound, what you like to do, and what you want to achieve in life. When your inner voice wakes up and starts talking, what is it saying? Then ask yourself, is it Truthful, Helpful, Inspiring, Necessary, and Kind (THINK)?

If not, challenge the inner voice and find something to say that is true, helpful, inspiring, necessary and kind (say something THINK). Here are some questions for you to answer:

1. **What's true about me?** *eg. I want to feel better*
2. **What is helpful for me to hear right now?** *eg. I have great potential*
3. **What can I say to inspire in myself self-compassion?** *eg. I won't give up on you*
4. **What is necessary for me to hear so I can feel better?** *eg. You have what it takes to break free*
5. ***What is something* kind I can say to myself?** *eg. You have beautiful eyes*

Self-love is, talking to and about yourself with nothing less than kindness and care. If you could use a break from all the harsh judgement you direct at yourself, here are quick ways to self-love:

Accept

Accept yourself, body, mind, soul, emotions and sensations, whether you feel sad, angry, unhappy with yourself, or lost. These do not define who you are as a person. Everyone feels that way sometimes. The important thing is that you don't stay there but love yourself enough to pick yourself up and do better next time.

Acknowledge and be proud of what you are good at

Everyone is excellent at something. Each person is unique in their own way. Think about what you enjoy. Think about what you're able to do to make others happy. Think about all the things you're good at, even the small ones. Please, take into account all you like about yourself and celebrate it. Don't compare your successes with other people's.

Don't rely on others to feel good about yourself

Other people do not define your worth. People are who they are, all on their own journey of self-discovery. Some are consciously doing it. Some are lost and doing what they think is best. Their perspective can never be the same as yours. Your perspective is unique to you alone, so there is no need to put others on a pedestal or wait for their approval. You are the only one who can assign yourself worth. Remind yourself that no matter what happens or whoever says anything, your self-esteem will remain solid and impenetrable.

Self Hypnosis

> *Give me a child until he is seven years old and I will show you the man (or woman).*
>
> — St Ignatius Loyola

95% of the outcome of your life comes from your subconscious program. Most of your programming around social anxiety was likely formed in your early childhood, between zero and seven years old, when your conscious mind has not yet developed. So, your subconscious mind was all there was. Your subconscious mind is like a sponge that only absorbs information; it cannot analyse. So, a child accepts what you tell them without question, and that information becomes their belief and reality. So, if you were told you were stupid, shy, that you are not a people person, or even that you are terrified of groups of people, that becomes your belief. Even if you heard a parent or an adult you look to for care and love saying and behaving in a manner that inspired fear, you would copy those behaviours and make them your own as a child.

At this tender age, a child's brain is in a state of hypnosis. The brain waves are slower. Refer back to chapter 4, Diagram 5. Children this young, operate at the level of Theta brain waves. This hypnotic state is the subconscious level of brain activity. To change anything subconsciously, you need to access this level of mind. Don't freak out though; it's not as complicated as it sounds. We all do it every day as we go to sleep and before we wake up. This level of mind can also be induced through meditation and or hypnosis. In my opinion, self-hypnosis is a form of meditation. For the meditation exercise and free meditation from Thashna Walsh Lifestyle Therapy, see chapter 4.

Like meditation, for self-hypnosis to be effective, you must enter into a slower brain wave frequency, which simply means calming your mind right down using the breathing techniques you have learned in this book. Letting go of all your senses in the external world and focusing your attention inside of you, going 'within'. Inside you is a place, black as space and void of anything but stillness, peace and pure love. It will take some practise to get there, so continue practising your breathing and following the guided hypnotic meditation to get you there. The idea is to get to this place of deep relaxation while bringing awareness to letting go of the anxiety, feeling it dissolve, fade, release and leave your body. Once you have allowed yourself to let go, allow the feeling of love and gratitude to flood your body, changing your energy to what it naturally wants to be, big, bold and free. Let warm light energy consume you as you breathe deep and remain totally chilled. It will feel strange because it's new and different. You may even resist it, and that's ok at first. That only means you need more practice. So, keep practising. The key is learning to surrender into yourself and trust yourself through the process. *Allow yourself to let go.*

There are three stages of practice I recommend when under self-hypnosis or meditation.

1. *Nothingness and rewire:* the stage where you let go into the void of pure relaxation and nothingness, trusting the energy and love of the universe inside you and all around you to harmonise and return you back to your true self.
2. *Aligning and illuminating the energy centres:* this stage restores the vibrance of your energy centres and energy field. So you may be free from all that holds you back, setting you free to open up to your extraordinary life.
3. *Creation and power:* the stage where you create the life you want for yourself while in this state of pure and deep relaxation. Successful, bold, strong, loving, unlimited.

Does this sound far-fetched for you, or even a little crazy? It's different, yes, which is why it feels unfamiliar. Trust your instincts that have brought you this far. God, The Universe, Lifeforce, Source, The Force, whatever you call it, the energy that creates life within and around you, already knows how to heal and guide you back to yourself. Nothing outside of yourself can get you back to where you intrinsically belong. All you need to do is relax, allow, surrender and be at one with your life Source again as you were when you were being created within your mother's womb. Trust that your nervous system, which has the blueprint for your whole, unlimited self, also has the means to restore, regenerate, reactivate and reclaim your mental and physical well-being.

It's not going to happen after a few times doing it. You will need to commit to the 21/90-day rule. The rule encourages doing your self-hypnosis, meditation, affirmation, etc. daily for a minimum of 21 days for new neural networks in the brain to start forming and another 90 days for them to hard-wire for permanent change (Dispenza 2012). After 3 to 4 months of doing this daily and correctly, you will be stunned at who you have become. You will ask yourself, who is this naturally chatty, fun, happy and free-spirited person? That is precisely what happened to me. So what are you waiting for?

Chapter 8
Thashna Walsh Lifestyle Therapy (TWLT)

TWLT was founded on the premise that we were all born to explore and experience life; we are meant to have fun along the journey, learning as we grow in strength and wisdom. While on the journey, we share that experience and wisdom along the way to lessen each other's burdens while guiding one another to freedom. TWLT started as a blog which rapidly morphed into a place where people could come and transform their fears into freedom. Freedom to be who they feel deep down they are but have been buried under so much misguided thinking. At TWLT, fully qualified RTT Therapists and Clinical Hypnotherapist take their clients on a very short journey back to themselves, confident and free, with the use of the technique of Rapid Transformational Therapy (RTT)

About RTT

For the determined, like myself, doing your meditation and self-hypnosis and the other exercises in this book will work brilliantly as long as you persevere. That is how I overcame the anxiety I suffered from. Understandably, others may need added assistance to get to the root cause of issues causing social anxiety. Founded by the brilliant Marisa Peer, RTT is a fast-growing and rapid therapy designed to transform and release you from social anxiety and numerous other issues that keep you stuck in your life in 1 to 3 sessions. It focuses on the individual's potential and uncovering what is blocking them from being their best, happy and free.

Hypnosis is used to get you to a state of relaxation to access your subconscious mind, where you store the programs of social anxiety. Once the RTT therapist helps you uncover the root cause of why you hold on to anxiety, they will help you release it, reframe it and replace it with who you decide you truly are. A bespoke recording is done for you during your session. This recording is key to replacing the subconscious issue that kept the anxiety program running in your subconscious mind. Listening to this recording for 21-90 days will bring about extraordinary changes within you which will change your life. You will feel great in your skin again, and nothing will stop you from shining bright and being all you were meant to be.

As you know, this is my field of expertise and my team, and I will be happy to help you should you choose to have someone help you directly. We are an online clinic, so geography is no problem. All the RTT therapists at TWLT have been trained personally by Maris Peer and continue to grow in expertise to suit the needs of the growing many.

Please visit our website https://www.thashnawalsh.com for further information about RTT and merchandise such as hypnotic meditations and books.

You may also, from the website, book a free Discovery call. A free 30-minute consultation with an RTT therapist on Zoom to learn how we can help you.

If you are 16 or younger, please ask your parents or guardian to book for you.

Join our Facebook Group, a community of people like you that want answers, support and to find their true selves again or for the first time and be the person they want to be without the burden of social or any form of anxiety.

Follow us on Facebook. Stay grounded and reminded along the journey of what you stand for and gently yourself back to where you want to be.

Follow us on Instagram. Again, stay grounded and reminded along the journey of what you stand for and gently guide yourself back to where you want to be.

Let's wrap this book up now, as you have all you need to be the boss of your life.

Conclusion

You have got this!

> *You can't go back and change the beginning but you can start where you are and change the ending*
>
> — C.S. LEWIS

Don't force yourself outside your comfort zone at the cost of your mental well-being. Instead, stay inside your comfort zone and learn who you are; love who you are as you grow into the best version of you. Growth does not happen by force but by flow, persistence and love. As you get inspired, your comfort zone will widen to envelop the world.

You have learned that understanding how your mind works is the key that unlocks everything. You know now how crucial your thoughts are and how they create your life, good or bad, is your choice. So, anxiety now makes sense, and at the same time, feels irrelevant. But that's cool because you have the tools to fiercely, yet, gracefully eradicate it and restore your natural, peaceful balance.

Start slowly, take little steps, and pace yourself. Use the exercises in this book to understand yourself and learn your threshold, and gently, one step at a time, ease past each of them. You are who YOU say you are. See yourself how you want to be seen; fun, outgoing, spontaneous, open and curious to know more about who you are and your incredible potential. It's your choice how you live the rest of your life.

Remember to be patient with yourself. If you come up against resistance, breathe, take a step back, assess the situation and go for it again as you adjust the strategy for success. You will persevere because 'giving up' is no longer in your vocabulary or your energy. Have you ever seen a child learning to walk, having fallen down a few times, then decided to give up? Of course not! Then why would you, when you know freedom from social anxiety is only practice steps away? Some days will be more challenging than others of course but remember; there is no growth without these challenges, big and small. You'll be ready to cope once you learn and keep in mind the grounding and breathing techniques learned.

Once you adopt the helpful coping tools and strategies, you will challenge negative thoughts and banish them rather than letting them own you. Your confidence will automatically grow as you practice. Soon enough, you will be able to open your eyes to the proof that you feel better and are free to be more of you. Most importantly, while practising the techniques, be kind to yourself as you would to someone you care about. If you can't say something kind about yourself in challenging times, try to be still and say nothing at all; remembering, your thinking needs more work.

The people you look up to (or admire) for their upbeat, outgoing nature are often the kindest to themselves and don't get stuck over their blunders. They understand that the journey through life brings variety, and they use it to learn, grow, become stronger and stay free. Absolutely do not compare your successes with others. You are unique and have your own journey to explore, so be excited. You've taken a giant leap by choosing this comprehensive book to work on overcoming social anxiety and being your true self, unhindered and happy regardless of what you face. So, see yourself the way you want to be seen, and progress will follow. Give yourself a huge praise my friend. The only way from here is up, above and beyond. You should be incredibly proud.

One final note. Reading the information in this book and understanding it is one thing. But that alone will not create the change you seek. You will need to actively participate in your transformation. For transformation to take place, you will need to integrate the lessons into your body (subconscious mind); only then will you automatically feel and express the changes in your life. Changes have to come from the inside out because what you put in is always reflected on the outside. Just like going to the gym to work out requires repetitive action to see results, your emotional strength and well-being require the same attention. Your brain learns by repetition; there is no other way. Practice makes progress, and I know you are capable, and by now, so should you.

Congratulations on completing this book. That's pretty radical. I believe in you and I am so happy for you; go do amazing things now that you remember who you are.

Please leave a review: To help others find the help they need to rid themselves of this awful disorder Social Anxiety, please leave your review on how the book has helped you. Your review and that of others will help many sufferers come across this book and therefore be able to make use of its valuable information. Thank you for taking the time to do this.

About Author

Dr Thashna Walsh

I was born and grew up on the beautiful island of Jamaica, and at the age of 21, I moved to the UK. After having a very stressful childhood, I struggled with social anxiety. I grew up overcompensating to fit in and appear normal. The perpetual stress led to a heart condition, Supraventricular Tachycardia (SVT). I read many books and did lots of courses to overcome the anxiety and the depression that came with it. Because I always wanted to help others like myself to free themselves from the pain I had experienced, I studied for a degree in Biochemistry and Physiology and then a second degree to become a Doctor of Chiropractic. I exposed myself to countless social situations, and in those moments, though I felt like I was dying, I had to train myself to be bold for my daughter.

Also, I couldn't allow anxiety to win because I knew I had to raise a bold and happy child. I also felt I was meant to do more with my life, so hiding away was not an option. I had many mentors, some of whom inspired me through their words in person, books, and courses, which kept me pressing forward to reach a higher version of myself. It took years of persevering and pushing to become more open and believe in myself. My heart got worse after experiencing some stressful results from choices I had made, so surgery was advised. I did not want this and opted to find a natural way to heal my heart. I understood that stress and anxiety were the cause of this condition, so I set out to heal my heart by natural means. After delving deep into some training on how the mind works and how it affects my body, I soon learned about who I was and how to embrace and love myself; I taught myself how to calm my mind through meditation. After adopting these new principles in my life, I broke through and never looked back. The SVT became significantly less, and I saw massive social changes in myself. I became happier and more at home in my own skin. Talking to people was no longer an issue. I was even having fun talking in groups of people and giving presentations. It was weird watching myself transform before my own eyes. I loved it.

As a chiropractor, helping my patients was very fulfilling. However, I found that though I was helping them physically and mentally, the tools I had to help them mentally were limited. I was always searching for ways to improve myself, and as I grew, I was compelled to share with others and help them get through the emotional pain they went through too. After 20 years of being a chiropractor, I discovered Rapid Transformational Therapy (RTT) and became an RTT therapist and a Clinical Hypnotherapist. I was blown away by its fast and deep effectiveness. I found it to be the therapy I wish I had when I was younger. I could have saved myself years of heartache and struggle.

I have focused on teenagers for this book because I wish I had this wisdom in my teens that I have now; it would have saved years of future pain and struggle. The last thing any teenager needs is a condition that blocks them from moving into their life fully open to find their way. So many are dismissed as just being teenagers without a single thought about their struggles. Though this book can help anyone with social anxiety, I dedicate it to teenagers because they need someone in their corner that supports them powerfully and positively through this condition. They no longer need to feel they have to hide and suppress themselves to survive. I can now guide them to the help they need in a short time so they can move on with their lives unhindered and free.

Power Tools

The Exercise index and checklist

Tick, "Yes, I've mastered this"

❏ Exercise 1: What ifs Chapter 1
❏ Exercise 2: Praise time Chapter 1
❏ Exercise 3: Tell your best self-story Chapter 1
❏ Exercise 4: Guide your imagination Chapter 2
❏ Exercise 5: Grounding Chapter 2
❏ Exercise 6: Visualise to actualise Chapter 2
❏ Exercise 7: Off the trigger 5-4-3-2-1 Chapter 3
❏ Exercise 8: Take out the adversary Chapter 4
❏ Exercise 9: Let's meditate Chapter 4
❏ Exercise 10: Positive Affirmations Chapter 5
❏ Exercise 11: Avoidance out Chapter 5
❏ Exercise 12: Let's dance Chapter 5
❏ Exercise 13: Breathe to thrive Chapter 6
❏ Exercise 14: Strength to strength Chapter 7
❏ Exercise 15: Anxiety Reappraisal Chapter 7
❏ Exercise 16: Body Scan Chapter 7
❏ Exercise 17: THINK Chapter 7

Resources and Notes

- Anderson, E. (2013). Effects of exercise and physical activity on anxiety. Frontiers in Psychiatry. https://www.frontiersin.org/articles/10.3389/fpsyt.2013.00027/full
- Babson, K. (2010). A Test of the Effects of Acute Sleep Deprivation on General and Specific Self-Reported Anxiety and Depressive Symptoms: An Experimental Extension. J Behav Ther Exp Psychiatry. https://www.ncbi.nlm.nih.gov/pmc/articles/PMC2862829/
- Bagatini, S. (2022). Higher Consumption of Fruit and Vegetables Is Associated With Lower Worries, Tension and Lack of Joy Across the Lifespan. Frontiers in Nutrition. https://www.frontiersin.org/articles/10.3389/fnut.2022.837066/full
- Baladron, J. (2020). Habit learning in hierarchical cortex–basal ganglia loops. European Journal of Neuroscience, 52(12). https://onlinelibrary.wiley.com/doi/full/10.1111/ejn.14730
- Bargh, J. (2008). The Unconscious Mind. Perspect Psychol Sci. https://www.ncbi.nlm.nih.gov/pmc/articles/PMC2440575/
- Brooks, A (2013) Get Excited. Journal of Experimental Psychology: General 2013 American Psychological Association
- Carvalho KMB, Ronca DB, Michels N, et al. Does the mediterranean diet protect against stress-induced inflammatory activation in european adolescents? The helena study. Nutrients. 2018;10(11):1770.

Resources and Notes

- Dispenza, J. (2012) Breaking the Habit of Being Yourself: How to Lose Your Mind and Create a New One. pg 204.
- Dispenza. J. (2007) Evolve Your Brain: The Science of Changing Your Mind. pg 329-330.
- Donner, J., & Pirkola, S. (2008, October). An Association Analysis of Murine Anxiety Genes in Humans Implicates Novel Candidate Genes for Anxiety Disorders. Biological Psychiatry.
- Granic, I. (2020). Beyond Screen Time: Identity Development in the Digital Age. Psychological Inquiry. https://www.tandfonline.com/doi/full/10.1080/1047840X.2020.1820214
- Heartmath. https://www.heartmath.org/resources/solutions-for-stress/increasing-energy/
- Hawkins, D. (2014). Power vs Force: The Hidden Determinants of Human Behavior.
- Murphy, J. (1963). The Power of Your Subconscious Mind.
- Kafka, F., & Bauer, F. (1973). Letters to Felice. Schocken Books Incorporated.
- Kiecolt-Glaser, J. (2011). Omega-3 supplementation lowers inflammation and anxiety in medical students: A randomized controlled trial. Brain, Behavior, and Immunity. https://www.sciencedirect.com/science/article/abs/pii/S0889159111004685?via%3Dihub
- Lipton, B. (2015). The Biology of Belief: Unleashing the Power of Consciousness, Matter and Miracles.
- Maekawa, M. (2021). Physical and psychological effects of postural educational intervention for students experienced school refusal. Current Psychology. https://link.springer.com/article/10.1007/s12144-021-01677-9

- Study Sheds New Light on Brain's Source of Power. https://www.urmc.rochester.edu/news/story/study-sheds-new-light-on-brains-source-of-power
- Peer, M. (2018). I Am Enough: Mark Your Mirror And Change Your Life.
- Peer, M. (2022). Tell Yourself A Better Lie: Use the power of Rapid Transformational Therapy to edit your story and rewrite your life.
- Schoenfeld, T. (2013). Physical Exercise Prevents Stress-Induced Activation of Granule Neurons and Enhances Local Inhibitory Mechanisms in the Dentate Gyrus. Journal of Neuroscience. https://www.jneurosci.org/content/33/18/7770
- Sousa, A. (2011). Freudian Theory and Consciousness: A Conceptual Analysis. Mens Sana Monogr. https://www.ncbi.nlm.nih.gov/pmc/articles/PMC3115290/
- A Netflix Documentary: The Social Dilemma.

Notes

Notes

Notes

Notes

Notes

Printed in Great Britain
by Amazon

20505864R00129